THE POWER OF RADICAL SELF-LOVE

UNLEASH YOUR INNER WARRIOR USING 4 DYNAMIC
MODALITIES! BECOME FEARLESS AND
UNAPOLOGETIC WITH PURE CONFIDENCE,
EMOTIONAL STRENGTH, AND LASTING SELF-
COMPASSION

LEIGH W. HART

CONTENTS

MODALITY FOUR
Narrative Therapy

My Gift to You!

Bonus #1

Customized Worksheets:

Elevate your journey with a **customized collection** of **110+ journal pages and interactive worksheets** that have been designed to complement the steps, journal prompts, and exercises discussed in this book perfectly.

BENEFITS:

- Print multiple copies of repeatable exercises.
- Create a private journal with the book's 150+ prompts.
- Increase your commitment to the exercises.
- Counselors, therapists, and coaches can share printed copies with clients.

Go to:

SelfLove.LeighWHart.com

to receive your BONUS printable support materials.

My Gift to You!

Mastering the Art of Time Management Workbook:

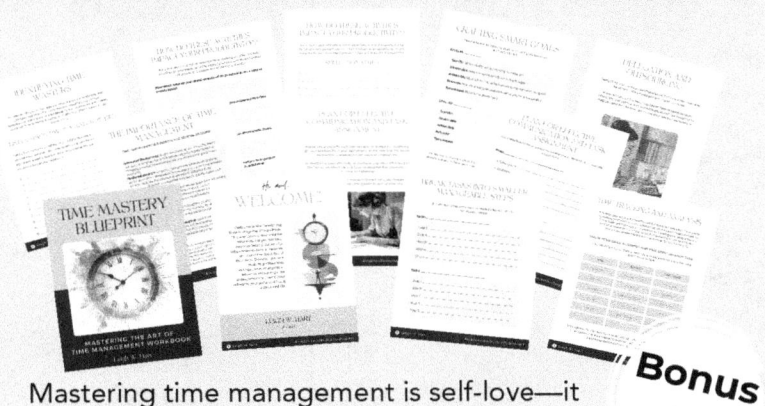

Mastering time management is self-love—it prioritizes well-being, reduces stress, and makes room for rest, growth, and fulfilling activities.

Bonus #2

The Wheel of Life Workbook:

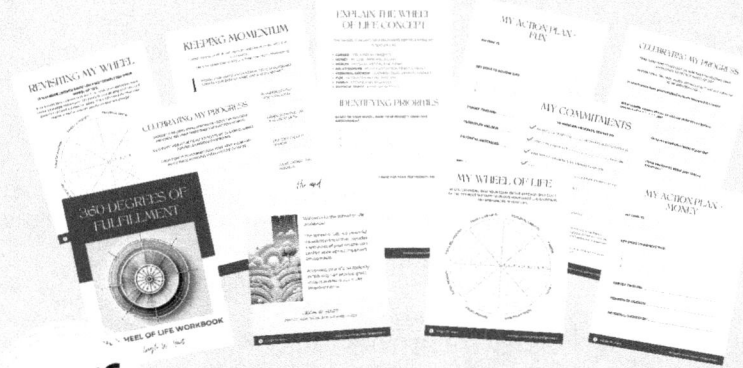

Bonus #3

The Wheel of Life is a powerful visualization tool that provides a snapshot of your satisfaction, balance, and growth across eight key areas of life.

Go to:

SelfLove.LeighWHart.com

to receive your BONUS printable support materials.

TRIGGER WARNING

This book, *The Power of Radical Self-Love,* explores topics that may be sensitive for some readers. It includes discussions on:

- Emotional challenges, such as self-doubt, anxiety, and feelings of unworthiness.
- Past traumas and how they may impact self-esteem and personal growth.
- Exercises that encourage self-reflection, which may bring up difficult emotions or memories.

The content is designed to provide support and healing, but it may stir up emotions as part of the process toward self-love and compassion. Please proceed at your own pace and seek additional support if needed.

MEDICAL DISCLAIMER

The information provided in *The Power of Radical Self-Love* is for educational and informational purposes only and is not intended as a substitute for professional medical advice, diagnosis, or treatment.

Always seek the advice of your physician, therapist, or other qualified health provider with any questions you may have regarding a medical condition or mental health concern. Never disregard professional medical advice or delay in seeking it because of something you have read in this book.

The author and publisher are not responsible for any adverse effects, results, or consequences arising from the use of this book or its contents. If you are in crisis or feel unsafe, please contact a healthcare professional or a crisis hotline in your area immediately.

INTRODUCTION

To love oneself is the beginning of a lifelong romance. –Oscar Wilde

If you're holding this book, there is a chance you've been feeling a little lost, a little stuck, or maybe just a little out of tune with the person you see in the mirror. I've been there too. Life has a way of piling on expectations, doubts, and chaos until you barely recognize yourself beneath it all. I'm here to remind you that you're not broken. You don't need fixing. What you need is a guide, a friend, and maybe a gentle nudge to help you uncover the amazing, resilient, and beautiful soul you already are. That's where this book comes in.

Unlike other self-help books that leave you with a mountain of advice but no roadmap, this book is your personal toolkit for building unstoppable confidence, emotional freedom, and lasting self-compassion. Together, we'll dive into four powerful modalities—mindfulness-based stress reduction (MBSR), dialectical behavior therapy (DBT), narrative therapy, and art therapy. Don't worry if these sound new or intimidating. Each one brings something unique to the table, and they're all designed to meet you exactly where you are on your journey.

You're here because you're ready to rediscover the spark that makes you, well, *you*. Maybe you've felt disconnected, weighed down by self-doubt, or overwhelmed by life's messy moments. Maybe you're curious about different therapeutic approaches but don't know where to start. Whatever brought you here, this book has you covered, welcome.

Why This Book Is for You

In these pages, you'll find:

- Shortcuts to self-love that actually work. No fluff, just practical tools you can use right now to feel more connected to yourself and your life.
- Guided exercises from four therapeutic modalities, tailored to help you build emotional resilience, trust your inner wisdom, and create a life you love.
- A step-by-step journey that doesn't overwhelm but empowers, with bite-sized practices you can easily fit into your day.

Let's briefly meet the four modalities that will guide us:

- **Mindfulness-based stress reduction (MBSR):** Have you ever wished you could turn down the volume of your racing thoughts? MBSR teaches you how to find calm in the chaos, helping you live more fully in the present moment.
- **Dialectical behavior therapy (DBT):** Life can be messy, but DBT gives you tools to handle it with grace. From

managing intense emotions to building healthier relationships, it's like a life-skills class for your soul.

- **Art therapy:** Don't worry, you don't need to be an artist. This modality taps into your creativity to help you express emotions, process your experiences, and reconnect with your inner self in ways words sometimes can't.
- **Narrative therapy:** Your life is a story, and you're the author. Narrative therapy helps you rewrite the scripts that no longer serve you, empowering you to reclaim your narrative and own your truth.

What You'll Get Out of This Journey

By the time you finish the final page, you'll walk away with:

- **Unshakable self-love:** A deep sense of acceptance that makes you your own biggest supporter, no matter what life throws your way.
- **Emotional freedom:** Tools to manage self-doubt, uncertainty, and overwhelm so you can approach challenges with confidence and calm.
- **Inner peace:** Practical techniques to help you recenter, reconnect, and cultivate tranquility amidst the chaos of daily life.
- **A personalized toolbox:** Exercises and strategies you can return to any time, blending the best of the four modalities into your unique self-care routine.

This isn't just a book—it's a conversation between us. I'll guide you, cheer you on, and sometimes make you laugh because self-love doesn't always have to be so serious, right? You'll feel supported, understood, and empowered every step of the way.

To aid you further, I've created customized worksheets and journal pages available at SelfLove.LeighWHart.com. These printable tools are crafted to help you fully engage with the steps, exercises, and journal prompts in this book.

So, are you ready to peel back the layers of self-doubt, reconnect with your spark, and build a foundation of love so strong it'll carry you through life's highs and lows? If your answer is even a hesitant yes, then let's get started.

This is your time to shine, and I'll be right here with you.

Let's begin.

CHAPTER 1: STEP ONE

YOUR HEALING BEGINS WITH YOU

 You can't go back and change the beginning, but you can start where you are and change the ending.

> — *C.S. LEWIS*

When was the last time you looked in the mirror and felt genuine love for the person staring back at you? Not the obligatory "Oh, I guess I look okay today" or the fleeting moment where your outfit finally clicks. I'm talking about a deep, no-holds-barred love—the kind you'd give your best friend when she's had a tough day or your child when they're showing you their latest masterpiece in macaroni art.

It's okay if your answer is, "Um... never?" Trust me, I've been there too. But here's the thing: your healing journey—yes, the one you've bravely decided to embark on—starts with this very concept. Loving yourself isn't some fluffy, feel-good slogan you stick on your bathroom mirror. It's the bedrock, the foundation, the sturdy platform that gives you the courage to stare down the hard stuff:

the trauma, the wounds, the patterns that don't serve you anymore. Self-love is where healing begins, where growth takes root, and where you learn to embrace *all* of who you are.

This chapter is here to help you get started. Together, we're going to explore what self-love really means. We'll talk about why it's so vital for your healing and how you can start showing up for yourself the way you've always deserved. It's not about being perfect—it's about being willing. Willing to believe that you are worth the love and care you so freely give to others.

By the end of this chapter, my hope is that you'll feel a little less like a stranger to yourself and a lot more like your own biggest supporter. Because nobody else can walk this path for you. You don't have to do it alone either—because you've got *you*. And I promise, that's more than enough to begin.

Take a deep breath. This is your time. Let's lay the foundation and start building a life that feels as good on the inside as it looks on the outside.

WHAT IT MEANS TO LOVE YOURSELF

Let's start with the heart of it all: self-love. It's more than a buzzword—it's a daily practice, a mindset, and a way of showing up for yourself that changes your life. Think of self-love as a sturdy four-legged chair. Each leg represents a necessary pillar: acceptance, appreciation, nurture, and transformation. If one leg is missing or wobbly, the whole chair becomes unstable. And who wants to sit on a wobbly chair? Let's explore each pillar so you can build your rock-solid foundation of self-love.

Acceptance: Loving the Real You

Acceptance is the cornerstone of self-love. It's about looking at your reflection and saying, "This is me, and that's more than okay." It means owning your quirks, your so-called flaws, and all the beautiful imperfections that make you, *you.*

If this feels hard, understand that this is normal. Many of us are professionals at accepting others but struggle to extend that same grace to ourselves. Picture someone you love—a best friend, partner, child, or even your pet. You don't demand perfection from them; you love them as they are. Now, imagine doing that for yourself. Scary? Maybe. Possible? Absolutely.

Acceptance doesn't mean you're stuck where you are—it means you're starting from a place of kindness instead of criticism. And here's a secret: acceptance often leads the way for the other pillars of self-love to fall into place.

Appreciation: Seeing Your Own Magic

Acceptance says, "I'm okay as I am." Appreciation takes it a step further and shouts, "I'm freaking amazing!" It's about celebrating the qualities that make you uniquely you—the things that light you up, make you laugh, or inspire others.

Think of how you'd rave about your best friend's sense of humor or your partner's kindness. Now, flip that energy inward. What's something fabulous about you? Maybe it's your ability to stay calm in chaos, your killer karaoke skills, or the way you always find the silver lining. Appreciation requires a bit of reflection, but trust me, it's worth the effort. Once you start seeing your own magic, the idea of loving yourself doesn't feel so far-fetched.

Nurture: Showing Up for Yourself Daily

Nurture is where self-love gets practical. It's not just about pampering yourself with spa days (although, yes, please do that too). Nurture is the everyday care you give yourself—eating foods that fuel you, moving your body, getting enough sleep, and setting boundaries.

How do you nurture a loved one? Do you make sure they're cared for, supported, and thriving? Self-nurture is about giving yourself that same reliable care. It's not glamorous, but it's essential. Small, consistent acts of nurture are like deposits in your self-love bank, and they build up over time.

Transformation: Becoming Your Best Self

If acceptance, appreciation, and nurture are about the present, change is about the future. It's the belief that you're not just good as you are—you're also capable of becoming even better. Transformation is the dream-chasing, goal-smashing, butterfly-emerging part of self-love.

Maybe change looks like starting a new career, leaving a toxic relationship, or finally running that marathon. Whatever it is, it's about investing in your potential and creating a life that aligns with your deepest desires. Transformation doesn't mean you're broken and need fixing; it means you love yourself enough to want the best for your future self.

Take away any one of these pillars, and self-love doesn't feel quite complete. Without acceptance, you might feel stuck in a loop of self-criticism. Without appreciation, you lose sight of your strengths and joys. Without nurture, you risk burnout. And without transformation, you miss out on the incredible life you're capable of building.

The beauty of these pillars is that they work together. Acceptance makes way for appreciation, appreciation fuels nurture, and nurture gives you the energy for transformation. Together, they form the foundation of a self-love practice that's unshakable.

So, let's start building your chair—one sturdy leg at a time.

WHY YOU SHOULD LOVE YOURSELF

Loving yourself isn't just a "nice-to-have." It changes everything— the magic ingredient that transforms how you show up in every part of your life. Think about it. When you truly love yourself, you stop seeking approval from the world and start finding it within. Self-love makes you feel good, builds your resilience while unlocking your potential, and gives you the courage to tackle life head-on.

Imagine waking up each morning with an unshakable sense of worth, knowing that you've got your own back no matter what. Self-love is the foundation of that confidence. It's what allows you to face hard truths, make bold moves, and nurture your emotional and physical well-being. When you start loving yourself, you're no longer your worst critic—you're your greatest ally. And trust me, that's a powerful shift.

Why Is It So Hard to Love Ourselves?

If self-love is so transformational, why does it feel so hard? Why can't we just wake up, look at ourselves, and say, "I'm freaking wonderful!" without any hesitation? The truth is, self-love doesn't come naturally for most of us—and that's not your fault. Let's unpack why:

- **The world teaches us to doubt ourselves:** We're told to believe in our worth—every book, self-help guru, and motivational quote says so. But then we step out into a world that seems determined to contradict that message. We're compared, criticized, and judged, and we start to internalize those voices. Maybe it started at home, with well-meaning but critical parents. Maybe it came from peers or teachers. And let's not forget the media, which floods us with impossible standards of beauty, success, and happiness. The result? We question our worth. We start believing that we're only lovable if we meet certain conditions—conditions set by a world that doesn't see us fully.

- **Negativity sticks like glue:** Our brains are wired to focus on the negative—it's called the negativity bias, and it's why one unkind comment can overshadow a dozen compliments. That time someone called you "stupid" or "ugly"? It stays with you, loud and clear, while the kind words fade into the background. No wonder we have a hard time believing in our worth.

- **We don't trust ourselves:** Even when a little voice inside whispers, "Maybe you're enough," we doubt it. We're so used to looking outward for validation—through relationships, achievements, or perfectionism—that we forget to listen to our own truth. We search for love everywhere except the one place it's always been: within ourselves.

How to Start Loving Yourself

The good news is self-love isn't some mystical quality you're either born with or not. It's a skill—a practice—that you can build. And while it's not always easy, it is absolutely possible. Let's start with a few simple steps:

- **Make a list of what you love about yourself:** Take a moment to celebrate you. What do you love about yourself? It could be your sense of humor, your empathy, your ability to cook a killer lasagna. Write it all down. Start small if you need to—even one thing is a win. Over time, you'll find more and more to add to the list. And on tough days, pull it out as a reminder of how amazing you already are.
- **Pay attention to your inner dialogue:** What do you say to yourself when no one's listening? If your self-talk is harsh or critical, start shifting it. When you catch yourself thinking, "I'm such a failure," replace it with, "I'm learning and growing." Be as kind to yourself as you would be to a loved one.
- **Start a gratitude practice:** Gratitude shifts your focus from what's missing to what's already there. Take time during your day to write down what you're grateful for. They don't have to be big—maybe it's your morning coffee,

a kind word from a friend, or the way the sun felt on your face. Gratitude helps you see the abundance in your life, and it's a powerful way to reconnect with yourself.

- **Accept and forgive:** You can't change the past, but you can change how you hold onto it. Forgive yourself for mistakes —real or perceived—and let go of the need to be perfect. It's through acceptance that we create space for healing and growth.

- **Nurture your body:** Loving yourself starts with taking care of your physical needs. Hydrate, nourish yourself with food that makes you feel good, and move your body in ways that bring you joy. It's not about achieving perfection; it's about showing yourself that you're worth the effort.

- **Dream big:** What do you want for your future? Let yourself imagine a life that feels good—not one that meets society's expectations, but one that lights you up. Self-love is about believing you deserve that life and taking steps to create it.

- **Surround yourself with inspiration:** Seek out books and communities that uplift you. Follow people who remind you of your worth and potential. Read words that inspire you to be kinder to yourself. Fill your world with messages that nourish your soul.

Self-love isn't a one-and-done thing. It's an empowered journey— a messy, beautiful process of learning to see yourself with fresh eyes. Some days will be harder than others, but every small step matters. Start where you are. Be patient. And most importantly, remember: you are worthy of the love you seek. Now, it's time to give it to yourself.

RIDDING YOUR HEART OF THE HURT

Carrying around unprocessed hurt is like trying to climb a mountain with a backpack full of rocks. You can do it, but it's exhausting, and it keeps you from moving forward freely. Trauma—the deep, emotional wounds we've endured—can feel like those rocks, weighing us down and getting in the way of loving ourselves. If you're going to create space for self-love to bloom, you've got to start by unpacking that backpack.

The process of healing from trauma isn't about pretending the pain doesn't exist. It's about acknowledging what's there—seeing it clearly for what it is—and taking steps to release its grip on your heart. Because the hurt you've experienced doesn't define you. But it can shape the way you see yourself, the way you show up in the world, and whether or not you allow love from yourself or others to take root.

How Trauma Impacts Your Sense of Self

Trauma has a way of whispering lies into our minds: You're not enough. You're broken. You're unworthy of love. Over time, these lies can shape how we see ourselves, eroding our confidence and self-worth. And the tricky part? Trauma often lives in our bodies and our behaviors, not just in our thoughts. It leaves a mark that shows up in ways we might not even realize.

Trauma can make you feel like a stranger to yourself like you're disconnected from the person you know you could be. It's not your fault, but it is your opportunity—to acknowledge the hurt and take back control of your narrative.

Signs You're Dealing With Trauma

Trauma shows up differently for everyone, but here are some common signs that it might still be impacting your life:

- **Physical signs:**
  - Chronic fatigue, muscle tension, or headaches
  - Difficulty sleeping or recurring nightmares
  - A feeling of being "on edge" or easily startled
- **Emotional signs:**
  - Feelings of shame, guilt, or unworthiness
  - Persistent sadness or numbness
  - Emotional outbursts, like anger or overwhelming anxiety
- **Behavioral signs:**
  - Avoidance of people, places, or situations that remind you of the hurt
  - Overworking or people-pleasing to distract yourself
  - Turning to unhealthy coping mechanisms, like overeating, substance use, or isolating yourself

Recognizing these signs isn't about labeling yourself as "traumatized." It's about understanding that these patterns are your brain and body's way of trying to protect you. They've been doing their best—but now it's time to teach them that you're safe and ready to heal.

Identifying and Overcoming Trauma Triggers

Triggers are those reminders of past pain, often popping up when you least expect them. A certain smell, a phrase, or even a tone of voice can transport you back to a moment of hurt. And while triggers can feel overwhelming, learning to identify and manage them is a powerful step toward healing. But how? Let's look at how to start:

- **Learn your triggers:** Start by noticing what sets off an intense emotional or physical reaction. Is it a specific place? A conversation topic? A particular time of year? Keep a journal to track these patterns—you might be surprised at what you uncover.
- **Create a grounding toolkit:** When triggers strike, having tools to bring you back to the present can make a world of difference. Try deep breathing exercises, holding onto a comforting object, or even repeating a mantra like, "I am safe, and I am here."
- **Give yourself grace:** Being triggered doesn't mean you're weak; it means you're human. Instead of beating yourself up, remind yourself that you're in the process of healing—and healing takes time.
- **Seek professional support:** Sometimes, the best way to tackle trauma is with the help of a therapist or counselor. Trauma-focused therapies like EMDR, somatic experiencing, or cognitive-behavioral therapy can help you process the pain and rewrite your internal narrative.

Making Space for Self-Love

Healing from trauma isn't about erasing the past—it's about reclaiming your power over it. When you start acknowledging your pain, you create room for something new to take its place: self-love, compassion, and the belief that you are enough. Here's how to begin:

- **Acknowledge the hurt:** It's okay to admit that what you went through was hard. Acknowledging your pain doesn't make you weak; it makes you courageous. Write it down, talk about it, or just sit with it for a moment. You can't heal what you won't face.

- **Challenge the lies:** Trauma might have taught you some unkind things about yourself. Start questioning those beliefs. Ask, "Is this really true, or is it just something I've been carrying?" Replace the lies with affirmations of your worth.

- **Celebrate the wins:** Healing doesn't happen overnight, and that's okay. Every time you face a trigger, show yourself compassion, or choose to love yourself despite the pain, you're making progress. Celebrate those moments— they matter.

Your trauma is part of your story, but it's not the final chapter. The pain you've carried doesn't have to keep defining you. When you acknowledge the hurt, understand its impact, and take steps to heal, you're creating space for a new, brighter version of yourself to emerge. You are worthy of that change, and you don't have to rush it.

INTERACTIVE ELEMENT: LOVE M(E)USINGS

Journal Prompts: Trauma Healing

These prompts are designed to help you gently reflect on your trauma, begin acknowledging your experiences, and identify steps toward healing. Grab a journal or print the customized journal pages from SelfLove.LeighWHart.com; take your time, breathe, and write freely.

1. What's one experience from your past that you've avoided thinking about? Why do you think it's difficult to face?
2. How has this experience shaped the way you see yourself?
3. What emotions come up when you reflect on this hurt?
4. What triggers remind you of this trauma? How do they make you feel?
5. How do you typically respond to these emotions or triggers? What might a healthier response look like?
6. Write a letter to your past self who went through the trauma. What would you say to comfort and support them?
7. What or who makes you feel safe today? How can you lean into that safety when you're struggling?
8. What does forgiveness mean to you? Is there anyone (including yourself) you're ready to forgive?
9. What's one small action you can take to create space for healing in your daily life?
10. If your trauma could speak, what would it say? What would you say back?
11. What have you learned about yourself through this healing journey so far?
12. What would a life free from the weight of this trauma look and feel like?
13. What support do you need to continue healing? How can you seek it?
14. What are three things you love about yourself despite what you've been through?
15. How can you show yourself compassion today?

Journal Prompts: Goal Setting for Self-Love

These prompts will help you clarify what self-love looks like for you and set achievable goals to nurture it.

1. What does self-love mean to you?
2. When do you specifically feel loved and supported? How can you create that for yourself?
3. What's one habit or belief that's standing in the way of self-love?
4. What is one small step you can take this week to show yourself love?
5. Imagine you're living a life full of self-love. What does your day look like?
6. What's a boundary you need to set to protect your peace?
7. How can you celebrate yourself more often?
8. What's one area of your life where you'd like to practice more self-care?
9. Who inspires you to be kinder to yourself? Why?
10. How can you make time for yourself in your busy schedule?
11. What's a fear that's been holding you back? How can self-love help you face it?
12. What's one thing you've always wanted to try but haven't because of self-doubt?
13. How can you make your environment (home, workspace, etc.) more nurturing for yourself?
14. What's a long-term goal you have for your self-love journey?
15. How will you know when you've made progress in loving yourself?

Activity: Crafting Your Personal Self-Love Mantra

A self-love mantra is a short, powerful phrase that grounds you to your worth and reminds you of your inherent value. Here's how to create your own.

Step 1: Reflect on Your Needs

Think about what you need most right now. Do you need more confidence? Acceptance? Forgiveness? Clarity? Write down a few words or phrases that resonate.

Step 2: Identify Your Core Values

What do you stand for? What do you want to embody as you grow? Words like strength, compassion, resilience, or joy might come to mind. Add these to your list.

Step 3: Choose Empowering Language

Your mantra should be written in a way that feels uplifting and positive. Start with phrases like "I am," "I embrace," or "I deserve." For example:

- Instead of "I won't be afraid," try "I am courageous."
- Instead of "I don't need validation," try "I am enough."

Step 4: Combine Your Ideas

Mix and match the words and concepts you've written down. Keep it short and easy to remember. For example:

- "I am worthy of love and kindness."
- "I choose peace over perfection."
- "I honor my journey and trust my growth."

Step 5: Test It Out

Say your mantra out loud. Does it feel true to you? If it doesn't resonate, tweak it until it feels like a warm hug from your future self.

Step 6: Put It to Use

Write your mantra down somewhere you'll see it daily—on your bathroom mirror, phone lock screen, or a sticky note on your desk. Repeat it to yourself in the morning, during stressful moments, or whenever you need a boost of love and encouragement.

Bonus Tip

Feel free to create multiple mantras for different situations! You can have one for confidence, one for resilience, and one for gratitude. The key is that each mantra serves as a loving reminder of who you are and the journey you're on.

Let your mantra be the heartbeat of your self-love practice—it's your personal anthem for embracing the incredible person you are.

You've taken some incredible steps on the path to self-love. By reflecting on your experiences, identifying what holds you back, and beginning to craft a practice that honors your worth, you've started building a foundation for a life filled with confidence, emotional freedom, and deep compassion for yourself. And the best part? This is only the beginning.

Now that you've begun the process of embracing yourself, it's time to add another powerful tool to your self-love arsenal: mindfulness. In the next chapter, we'll dive into mindfulness-based stress reduction (MBSR), a practice that helps you cultivate presence and peace, strengthening your relationship with yourself.

So take a deep breath, celebrate how far you've come, and get ready to explore the transformative power of mindfulness. You're on a beautiful, empowering path and the best is yet to come.

MODALITY ONE

MINDFULNESS-BASED STRESS REDUCTION
(MBSR)

CHAPTER 2: HEART-CENTERED CALM

ZEN AND THE ART OF LOVING YOURSELF

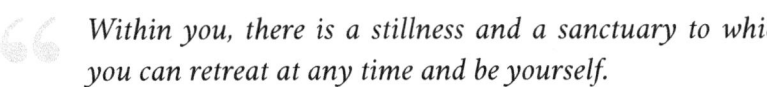 *Within you, there is a stillness and a sanctuary to which you can retreat at any time and be yourself.*

— *HERMANN HESSE*

I would like to ask yourself how often you feel caught in the relentless whirlwind life brings? The to-do lists that never seem to shrink, the constant pressure to be *on* for everyone else, and that voice in your head whispering, "Get with it, girl, you're not doing enough"? If this sounds familiar, take a deep breath (yes, right now—go ahead, I'll wait). Because the secret to untangling the chaos and finding your calm isn't hidden in some exotic retreat or locked inside the latest self-help fad. It's already within you, patiently waiting for you to pause and say, "Hi, I'm ready to choose me and love myself."

In this chapter, we're unveiling the beautiful, transformative practice of mindfulness-based stress reduction (MBSR). Don't worry; you don't need a yoga mat, incense, or the ability to sit still for hours on end. You just need a willingness to meet yourself where you are—messy emotions, busy brain, and all. Together, we'll explore how MBSR can help you hit the pause button, breathe through the noise, and create a sense of peace so solid it feels like coming home to your heart.

When you embrace this practice, you're managing stress and building a deeper, more loving relationship with yourself. You'll learn how to show up for *you*—not just when things are going smoothly, but especially when life feels like a never-ending obstacle course.

THE ANATOMY OF STRESS

Stress is your body's built-in alarm system, designed to keep you alert and ready to tackle challenges. At its simplest, stress is the physical and emotional response to a perceived threat or demand. This could be anything from a tight deadline to a difficult conversation with your partner. Stress itself isn't inherently bad—it's how your body mobilizes energy to respond when life gets messy. However, when stress becomes chronic or overwhelming, it stops being helpful and starts interfering with your well-being.

The stress response begins in your brain when it detects a potential danger. This activates your hypothalamus, which sends a distress signal to your adrenal glands, triggering the release of adrenaline and cortisol. These hormones increase your heart rate, sharpen your focus, and flood your muscles with energy to help you respond (*Stress*, 2022). It's your body saying, "I've got your back—let's get through this!" But when this response is stuck in the "on" position, your body and mind can pay the price, leading to fatigue, irritability, and even long-term health issues.

Types of Stress

Not all stress is created equal. Understanding the different types can help you recognize what you're dealing with and choose the best strategies to address it. Let's break it down (Tiwari, 2023):

- **Acute stress:** Think of acute stress as the sprinter of stress types—it comes on quickly, demands your attention, and is usually short-lived. This is the kind of stress you feel when you're running late, preparing for a big meeting, or swerving to avoid a car in traffic. It's your body's way of helping you stay sharp and reactive in the moment. Once the challenge passes, your stress levels return to baseline. While acute stress isn't necessarily harmful, frequent bouts can add up and start to take a toll.
- **Chronic stress:** Chronic stress is the marathon runner—persistent, exhausting, and much harder to shake off. It happens when you're exposed to stressors over a prolonged period, like ongoing financial struggles, a toxic work environment, or caregiving responsibilities. Unlike acute stress, which resolves after the event, chronic stress keeps your body's alarm system stuck in overdrive. Over time, it can lead to burnout, anxiety, depression, and physical health issues like heart disease or weakened immunity.
- **Episodic acute stress:** This happens if you often experience acute stress and can't seem to escape it. You might recognize it in that one friend who's always running late, missing deadlines, and overcommitted. It's the "chaos mode" of stress types, where the stress cycle repeats itself so often that it feels like a way of life. Without intervention, episodic acute stress can lead to serious emotional and physical strain.

- **Eustress:** Did you know that not all stress is bad? Eustress (think of it as "good stress") is the kind of stress that pushes you to grow, adapt, and perform at your best. It's the rush of energy you feel before tackling a big goal, starting a new project, or heading into an exciting life event like a wedding or promotion. Eustress keeps you motivated and resilient—proof that stress isn't always the enemy.
- **Emotional stress:** This stress type stems from interpersonal relationships, personal loss, or unresolved feelings. It's often tied to emotions like worry, sadness, or frustration. Left unchecked, emotional stress can snowball, affecting your mental and physical health.
- **Environmental stress:** This type of stress comes from your surroundings—think noise pollution, crowded spaces, or extreme weather. Even subtle environmental factors, like clutter or a chaotic household, can add to your stress load.

When you can identify the kind of stress you're facing, it becomes easier to manage. Acute stress might call for a quick breathing exercise, while chronic stress may require a more in-depth lifestyle overhaul. Eustress, on the other hand, is your friend—lean into it! Recognizing the anatomy of stress is how you start to tackle it with compassion and strength and use the tools we'll cover in the rest of this chapter.

How Do You Know You're Too Stressed Out?

In small doses, stress can be great, boosting your focus, performance, and even creativity. Think of it like a shot of espresso: Just enough gets you through the day, but too much leaves you jittery and overwhelmed.

However, there's a tipping point where stress stops being helpful and morphs into something much more harmful: chronic stress, otherwise known as bad stress. It's the kind of stress that doesn't clock out, keeping your body and mind in a constant state of overdrive. So, how do you know if your stress is the productive, short-term kind or the kind that's overstaying its welcome?

Normal Stress: The Quick Fixer

Normal stress is like that friend who shows up, makes a fuss for a minute, and then leaves before things get awkward. Your body is designed to handle it in bursts. Once the situation—say, catching a train or having a quick argument—is over, your autonomic nervous system kicks in, helping you calm down and reset.

Examples of normal stress include:

- **Before a big presentation:** You feel butterflies in your stomach, but they settle once you're rolling.
- **After an argument with a loved one:** Your heart races, and you feel warm, but you're back to normal soon after.
- **At the doctor's office:** You squeeze your eyes shut before a shot, but you're good to go afterward.
- **Rushing to catch a flight:** You feel tense racing through the airport, but relax once you're on the plane.

In these cases, your body bounces back relatively quickly. It's your stress system doing its job and then hitting "off" when it's no longer needed.

When Stress Overstays: Chronic Stress

Now chronic stress, on the other hand, is the clingy, never-ending houseguest of stress responses. Chronic stress happens when your body is constantly in fight-or-flight mode, unable to return to its usual routines like digestion, sleep, or even producing insulin properly. This can lead to some serious physical and emotional consequences over time, like burnout, anxiety, and even health issues such as high blood pressure, heart disease, and weakened immunity (Tiwari, 2023).

Unlike the short-lived bursts of normal stress, chronic stress keeps you in a state of physiological arousal. It's like your body's alarm system is stuck on snooze, constantly blaring but never really shutting off. Here are some signs your stress might be tipping into chronic territory:

- **Before a big presentation:** You're anxious and shaky for hours or even days leading up to it. You can't sleep, and your digestion is a mess.
- **After an argument:** You lose your appetite or feel irritable or depressed for a prolonged period.
- **At the doctor's office:** You avoid appointments entirely out of fear or find yourself dizzy or faint while you are there.
- **Before a flight:** You lose sleep the night before, worrying about everything from packing to delayed flights and even traffic.
- **After a long workday:** You turn to heavy drinking or binge-eating instead of decompressing in healthy ways.

The key to recognizing when stress becomes a problem is noticing how long it takes you to recover and how intensely you're reacting. Normal stress is like a quick rainstorm—you feel the splash, but then the sun comes back out. Chronic stress, on the other hand, is like a never-ending drizzle that soaks everything in its path.

Your body wasn't built to live in a constant state of alarm, and the good news is, it doesn't have to.

WRAPPING YOUR HEAD AROUND MINDFULNESS

Let's start with the basics: what *is* mindfulness, really? For years, I thought mindfulness was just a fancy way of saying, "meditate until your legs fall asleep" or "stare at a candle until you feel like a monk." Spoiler alert: it's not. Mindfulness is much simpler and way more forgiving. At its core, mindfulness is about being present—right here, right now—without judgment. It's noticing what's happening in your mind, body, and surroundings without immediately trying to fix, fight, or flee. Read that last bit again; it's important.

Picture your mind is like a chatty, hyperactive toddler. Mindfulness is the moment you gently take that toddler's hand and say, "Hey, let's sit down and just relax for a second." No chasing, no scolding, no bribing—just being. Sounds peaceful, right?

But why does this matter? Because life has a way of pulling us in a million directions, and when we're constantly rushing, worrying, or overthinking, we lose touch with ourselves. Mindfulness helps you hit the pause button and reconnect with the most important person in your life: you.

The Benefits of Mindfulness

Mindfulness is more than a feel-good trend; it's backed by science and can change how you handle stress, relationships, and even your own self-talk. Here's what mindfulness can do for you (*Mind-Body Connection: The Role of Meditation and Mindfulness*, 2023):

- **Reduce stress:** Mindfulness gives your overworked brain a breather. When you're fully present, your body's stress response has a chance to calm down, letting your nervous system return to its natural state of balance. It's like giving your brain a spa day. Sounds amazing, right?
- **Boost confidence:** When you're mindful, you're less likely to get caught up in negative thought loops like "I'm really sucking at life right now" or "Why did I say that?" Instead, you start to notice those thoughts for what they are—just thoughts—and let them pass without judgment.
- **Enhance emotional freedom:** Mindfulness helps you tune in to your emotions without being controlled by them. You'll start to respond to life's chaos with clarity and calm instead of reacting with panic or frustration.
- **Strengthen the mind-body connection:** Mindfulness grounds you in your body, helping you notice how your emotions and thoughts physically show up. That tight chest before a big meeting? That's stress. That warm glow after a hug? That's love. Understanding this connection helps you care for yourself more holistically.
- **Foster self-compassion:** When you practice mindfulness, you're practicing *noticing*—and that includes noticing how you talk to yourself. Over time, you'll catch those self-critical thoughts and replace them with kindness.

The Mind-Body Connection

Here's where it gets fascinating: your body and mind are always talking. Every thought, emotion, and experience leaves its mark on your physical self. Have you ever noticed how your shoulders creep up to your ears when you're stressed or how your stomach knots when you're anxious? Maybe your jaw is clenched during those tense family holiday dinners? That's the mind-body connection in action.

But it works both ways. Just as your mind influences your body, your body can influence your mind. When you focus on your breath, relax your muscles, or even just notice how your feet feel on the ground, you're sending signals to your brain that say, "Hey, we're safe. We can chill."

Mindfulness is the bridge between your mind and body. It helps you listen to what your body is telling you and respond with care, whether that's taking a break, asking for help, or simply breathing through a tough moment.

Mindfulness isn't about turning off your thoughts or floating on a cloud of eternal calm. It's about showing up for yourself—messy thoughts, wild emotions, and all—and finding peace in the present moment. It's a practice, not perfection.

When you welcome mindfulness into your life, you're learning to handle stress and learning to love yourself through it. And that, my empowered warrior, is where unstoppable confidence, emotional freedom, and lasting self-compassion begin. So, take a deep breath, let it out, and let's start building that connection between your mind and body. You're going to love what you discover.

MINDFULNESS-BASED STRESS REDUCTION (MBSR): YOUR GATEWAY TO CALM AND CLARITY

MBSR is one of those life-changing tools that feels like a secret you're finally being let in on. It's a structured program that takes the idea of mindfulness and turns it into a practical, science-backed way to manage stress, improve well-being, and reconnect with yourself. But what makes MBSR so impactful, and why has it become a cornerstone in stress reduction practices?

The History of MBSR

MBSR was developed in the late 1970s by Dr. Jon Kabat-Zinn at the University of Massachusetts Medical School. Kabat-Zinn, a molecular biologist and meditation practitioner, wanted to create a secular, science-based approach to mindfulness that anyone could use—no religious affiliation, incense, or chanting required (Mayer, 2022).

He started by teaching mindfulness to patients with chronic pain and stress-related conditions. The results were astounding: participants reported feeling calmer, more in control, and better equipped to handle their challenges. Since then, MBSR has been adopted worldwide, helping millions of people reduce stress and improve their quality of life (Mayer, 2022).

The Important Principles of MBSR

MBSR isn't about eliminating stress because life is always going to throw chaos at you. Instead, it's about changing how you relate to stress. Here are the core principles (Kriakous et al., 2020):

- **Awareness:** MBSR teaches you to become aware of your thoughts, emotions, and physical sensations without judgment. This awareness helps you catch yourself before stress spirals out of control.
- **Presence:** The program emphasizes living in the moment instead of dwelling on the past or worrying about the future. By focusing on the here and now, you give your mind a chance to rest.
- **Non-reactivity:** Instead of reacting impulsively to stress, MBSR helps you pause, breathe, and respond with intention. This can change how you handle challenging situations.
- **Acceptance:** MBSR encourages you to accept your experiences as they are without trying to push them away or change them immediately. This doesn't mean resignation—it means creating space for clarity and wise action.

What Are the Benefits of MBSR?

MBSR has a laundry list of benefits that touch almost every area of life. Here are just a few ways it can help (Kriakous et al., 2020):

- **Stress reduction:** MBSR lowers levels of cortisol, the stress hormone, helping you feel calmer and more centered.
- **Improved mental health:** It's been shown to reduce symptoms of anxiety, depression, and post-traumatic stress disorder (PTSD).
- **Better physical health:** MBSR can alleviate chronic pain, improve sleep, and boost immune function.

- **Enhanced focus and clarity:** Practicing mindfulness sharpens your attention and helps you stay present in the moment.
- **Greater emotional resilience:** MBSR helps you manage life's ups and downs with more grace and less overwhelm.
- **Increased self-compassion:** The program teaches you to treat yourself with the kindness and care you deserve.

Scientific Studies on MBSR

The beauty of MBSR is that it's not just feel-good fluff—it's backed by solid science. Here are some key studies that highlight its effectiveness:

- **Stress reduction:** A study published in *Psychological Science* found that MBSR participants showed significant reductions in stress and anxiety compared to control groups. Brain imaging revealed decreased activity in the amygdala, the brain's stress center (Hofmann et al., 2010).
- **Chronic pain management:** Research in *The Journal of Behavioral Medicine* found that MBSR significantly reduced pain intensity and improved quality of life for those with conditions like fibromyalgia and arthritis (Rosenzweig et al., 2010).
- **Mental health:** A meta-analysis in *JAMA Internal Medicine* (2014) concluded that MBSR is effective in reducing symptoms of anxiety, depression, and stress in clinical populations (Goyal et al., 2014).
- **Immune function:** A study in *Annals of Behavioral Medicine* found that MBSR enhanced immune response in participants, helping them fight off illness more effectively (Black & Slavich, 2016).

- **Workplace stress:** Research from the Journal of Adolescent and Youth Psychological Studies demonstrated that MBSR reduced burnout and improved job satisfaction in healthcare professionals—a group particularly prone to high stress (Hematian & Moraveji, 2023).

How MBSR Works in Practice

MBSR combines guided meditations, gentle movement, and mindfulness. You should do your best to commit to a daily mindfulness practice, learning how to incorporate mindfulness into your everyday life, which we will cover as we move through this book.

It's less about being still for hours on end and more about blending mindfulness into your day, from how you drink your morning coffee to how you handle a difficult conversation.

MBSR isn't a quick fix—it's a way of life. But with consistency, it can change the way you experience stress and life itself. When you strengthen the mind-body connection, MBSR gives you the tools to face challenges with confidence, compassion, and calm.

If you're ready to make peace with stress and build a deeper relationship with yourself, MBSR might just be what you've been looking for.

MBSR EXERCISES AND TECHNIQUES: QUICK TIPS FOR CREATING A MINDFULNESS HABIT

Building a mindfulness habit doesn't have to feel like climbing a mountain. It's about starting small, blending mindfulness into your everyday routines, and finding techniques that resonate with you. Here are some simple strategies to help you build greater presence and awareness as part of your daily life.

- **The one-minute pause:** Take one minute to focus on your breath or notice your surroundings. Whenever you feel rushed or overwhelmed, pause for a single minute. Pay attention to your breath, how your body feels, or the details in your environment. This brief moment of mindfulness can calm your nervous system and help you reset.

- **Mindful transitions:** Use transitions—like walking to your car or switching tasks—as moments to check in with yourself. Instead of rushing through these in-between moments, treat them as opportunities to pause, take a deep breath, and bring your attention to the present. For example, as you walk to your car, notice the sensation of your feet hitting the ground or the feel of the air on your skin.

- **Mindful breathing cues:** Use everyday cues—like a stoplight or a ringing phone—as a reminder to take a deep breath. Instead of letting these moments trigger impatience, use them as opportunities to practice mindfulness. Take a slow inhale and exhale before moving on.

- **Practice loving-kindness on the go:** Silently wish others well as you move through your day. For example, when you're stuck in traffic or waiting in line, take a moment to silently say, "May you be happy" to the people around you. This builds compassion and shifts your focus from frustration to kindness.

- **Start small and stay consistent:** Set a timer for just five minutes a day to practice mindfulness. You don't need to overhaul your life to build a mindfulness habit. Start small, stay consistent, and let the habit grow naturally. Over time, these small moments will add up to big changes in how you handle stress and show up for yourself.

Mindfulness is a skill, and like any skill, it gets stronger with practice. These simple techniques help you build awareness and presence without adding extra stress to your day. When you incorporate mindfulness into everyday moments, you're training your brain to focus, reframe, and respond with calm and clarity.

In the next chapter, we'll jump into specific exercises and meditation scripts to take your mindfulness practice to the next level. For now, take a breath, try one of these tips, and know that every small step brings you closer to greater peace and presence.

Interactive Element: Love M(e)usings – Journal Prompts for Presence

Journaling is one of the simplest and most powerful ways to deepen your mindfulness practice. It gives you a chance to pause, reflect, and connect with your thoughts and feelings in a meaningful way. These prompts are designed to help you step into the present moment, notice the beauty around you, and nurture a stronger connection with yourself.

Grab a journal or your printed journal pages from SelfLove.Leigh-WHart.com, find a cozy spot, and let's dive in:

1. **What made me smile today?** Reflect on even the tiniest moments of joy and how they made you feel.

2. **What is one thing I accomplished today that I'm proud of?** Focus on your wins, no matter how big or small they seem.

3. **If I could freeze one beautiful moment from today, what would it be? Why?** Capture a mental snapshot of something you'd like to hold onto.

4. **What is one thing my body did for me today that I'm grateful for?** Tune into your body's resilience and the ways it supports you.

5. **What is one thing I've been rushing through lately that deserves my full attention?** Explore how slowing down might change your experience.

6. **If I could thank one person, place, or thing today, what would it be?** Write a gratitude note to something or someone that positively impacted your day.

7. **What emotion am I feeling right now? Where do I feel it in my body?** Practice naming and noticing your emotions without judgment.

8. **What is one way I can show myself love and kindness today?** Create a plan to prioritize your well-being.

9. **If I could speak to my past self from this moment, what would I say?** Imagine giving your younger self a dose of encouragement or wisdom.

10. **What's one small thing in my life I've been taking for granted? How can I appreciate it more?** Bring attention to the overlooked gifts in your life.

11. **If today was a color, what would it be? Why?** Use imagery and creativity to explore your day's energy.

12. **What is one thing I can let go of that no longer serves me?** Identify what's weighing you down and imagine releasing it.

13. **What's one thing I'm looking forward to tomorrow?**
    Shift your focus to the positive and set an intention for the next day.

Your journal is a safe space where you can show up fully without filters or expectations. Let these prompts guide you toward presence, positivity, and self-discovery. There's no right or wrong way to do this—just write, reflect, and allow yourself to be exactly where you are. You're on a beautiful journey, one mindful moment at a time.

Take a moment to appreciate how far you've come already. You've created space for curiosity, calm, and self-awareness, and that's no small thing. These are the building blocks for the confidence, emotional freedom, and lasting self-compassion you deserve.

But this is just the beginning.

In the next chapter, we're diving deeper into the practical side of mindfulness with specific techniques to help you quiet the noise, clear the mental clutter, and feel more present in your daily life. Think of it as a toolkit for navigating stress and finding your calm —even on the busiest or most chaotic days.

Get ready to breathe, move, and release what no longer serves you. You're building something incredible here, one mindful moment at a time.

CHAPTER 3: BREATHING SPACE

MINDFULNESS MOVES TO CLEAR THAT MENTAL CLUTTER

 Sometimes, the most important thing in a whole day is the rest we take between two deep breaths.

— *ETTY HILLESUM*

You know that feeling when your mind feels like the junk drawer in your kitchen? You know it's full of useful stuff, but good luck finding the thing you actually need. That's what mental clutter feels like—an overwhelming mix of to-do lists, worries, and random thoughts that leave you spinning. Trust me, I've been there. Sometimes, it feels like my brain has about 47 tabs open, and none of them are responding.

But wouldn't it be empowering and relaxing to have a mind that feels as spacious and clear as a sunny sky? The path to get there isn't about adding more tasks to your already full plate. It's about slowing down and making room to breathe—literally and figuratively.

This chapter is your permission slip to pause and reclaim that mental breathing space. It's time to unveil the mindfulness practices inspired by MBSR. These are simple, effective moves to help you get out of your head and into the moment, wherever you are. No chanting required.

By the time we're done here, you'll have tools to quiet the chaos and reconnect with the present moment. You'll learn to welcome the beauty of now, let go of what doesn't serve you, and build a peaceful relationship with the one person you'll spend the rest of your life with—you. Let's clear the clutter and make some space to breathe. Ready?

CREATING A SERENE SPACE: YOUR MINDFUL SANCTUARY

Let's talk about creating a space where you can finally exhale—that magical corner of your world dedicated to meditating, slowing down, letting go, and reconnecting with yourself. Think of it as your personal oasis, where distractions are banished and peace takes center stage. Yes, you can totally carve out your serene space —even if it's just a cozy corner of your living room. In the next chapter, we will discuss how to create a safe space, but how are these different? Your "safe" space prioritizes emotional safety and expression, while a meditation space focuses on mindfulness and inner calm. A safe space adapts to the moment's emotional needs, whereas a meditation space is more fixed in its design and purpose. A safe space might involve others for support, while a meditation space is typically a solo environment.

When you create a dedicated meditation space, you're setting the stage—both physically and mentally—for a practice that supports your growth and well-being. It's not just about where you sit; it's about the energy you invite into that space. Here's why this matters:

- **Distractions? Bye-bye:** A meditation space helps you minimize the chaos, whether it's noise, clutter, or the endless pinging of your phone. This is your "Do Not Disturb" zone.
- **Your vibe, your rules:** From calming colors to candles or a plant named Fred, you can design this space exactly how you want. Make it yours.
- **Habit-building magic:** Practicing in the same spot every day creates consistency, which means you'll actually stick to it. Plus, over time, just seeing your meditation space will put you in the right mindset.

What Makes a Good Meditation Space?

A great meditation space is like a warm hug—it should feel safe, comfortable, and distraction-free. You don't need an entire room;

even a small, quiet nook can work wonders. Here's what to keep in mind:

- **Location, location, location:** Pick a spot that's quiet and preferably out of the way. If you can't escape the noise, grab some noise-canceling headphones or a white noise machine.
- **Comfort is key:** Add a soft cushion, a supportive meditation bench, or even a plush chair. Your back will thank you.
- **Let there be light:** Natural light is ideal, but if that's not an option, go for soft, warm lighting. Bonus points for candles—they're cozy and calming.
- **Decorate thoughtfully:** Think candles, calming artwork, or a small plant. Keep it simple and peaceful, but feel free to add your personal touch.

Step-by-Step: Build Your Meditation Space

Ready to create your sanctuary? Let's do this step by step:

1. **Pick the spot:** The first thing on the list is to find the perfect spot. Look for a place where you feel calm and undisturbed. A corner of your bedroom or even a spare closet can work.
2. **Clear the clutter:** Next, clear out the area. Remove anything that screams chaos (hello, unfolded laundry). Keep this space clean, simple, and free of distractions.
3. **Find your seat:** You don't want your Zen to be disturbed by discomfort, so next on the list is finding your seat. Try a plush cushion or a cozy chair, but make sure it's comfy enough for extended periods. Try a few options to find your perfect fit.

4. **Set the vibe:** Next, how do you want the space to feel? Remember, you want this area to exude calm. When you close your eyes and think of that word, what images do you see? This is different for everyone. Maybe that is a soft blanket, a picture of the beach, a vanilla-scented candle, or even turtle-shaped pillow (speaking from personal experience). Keep the colors and textures soothing.

5. **Bring in essentials:** Finally, wrap it up with the essentials. Consider tools like a meditation timer, a sound machine, a meditation app, a singing bowl, crystals, or incense. These little touches can help set the mood and keep you focused.

Creating a serene space isn't just about aesthetics. It's about building a haven that supports your mental well-being. This little corner of your life can help you focus better, stress less, and dive deeper into your mindfulness techniques. It's your space to breathe, let go, and find that peaceful connection with yourself.

So, roll up your sleeves and start creating your meditation sanctuary. Trust me, you're going to love what it does for your mind—and your soul.

MBSR MINDFULNESS TECHNIQUES

MBSR techniques are like a gentle reset button for your mind and body, helping you manage life's chaos with more calm, clarity, and compassion. These practices aren't about perfection—they're about presence, giving you tools to slow down, embrace each moment, and reconnect with yourself in a meaningful way.

Breathwork: MBSR Mindful Breathing Script

Mindful breathing is the cornerstone of many mindfulness practices, and for a good reason—it's simple, accessible, and endlessly grounding. Your breath is always with you, ready to guide you back to the present moment. Whether your mind feels like a swirling storm or a calm sea, mindful breathing can anchor you. Here's a guided script to help you practice MBSR mindful breathing:

1. **Settle in:** Find a quiet, comfortable space (like your new meditation space). Sit in a way that feels supportive and comfortable. Rest your hands in your lap or on your knees. Allow your spine to be tall but not rigid—imagine a string gently pulling you upward. Close your eyes.
2. **Notice your body:** Take a moment to notice how your body feels. Feel the connection between your body and the surface beneath you. Scan your body briefly, letting go of tension as you exhale.
3. **Focus on the breath:** Bring your attention to your breathing. You don't have to change it—just take notice. Feel the air entering your nostrils, moving through your body, and flowing out. Where do you feel it most clearly? Your chest? Your belly? Your nose? Let your awareness settle there.
4. **Count the breath:** If your mind wanders (and it will), gently guide it back by silently counting your breaths. Inhale: "One." Exhale: "Two." Continue counting up to ten, then begin again. This is just a tool—feel free to drop it if it feels distracting.
5. **Handle distractions with kindness:** If your mind drifts (hello, grocery list or stressful meeting), simply notice the thought and let it go. Imagine it as a cloud passing in the

sky. Gently return your focus to your breath. No judgment —it's all part of the practice.

6. **Expand awareness:** After several minutes, you might broaden your focus to include the sensations of your whole body breathing. Notice how the breath connects you to the present moment.

7. **Close the practice:** When you're ready, bring your awareness back to your surroundings. Stretch your fingers and toes, and open your eyes if they were closed. Take a moment to acknowledge yourself for practicing. Notice how you feel.

BREATHING TECHNIQUES FOR STRESS RELIEF

Sometimes, life gets overwhelming, and you need a quick, effective way to calm your mind and body. Breathwork techniques can be your go-to tools for managing stress and tension. Here are a few simple, science-backed techniques to try (Cronkleton, 2024).

Box Breathing (Square Breathing)

How it works: This technique involves breathing in a rhythmic pattern to calm the nervous system and focus your mind.

Steps:

1. Take a deep breath in through your nose.
2. Hold for a count of four.
3. Blow out through your mouth for a count of four.
4. Hold for a count of four.

Repeat this cycle for one to five minutes. Imagine tracing the sides of a square as you breathe.

4-7-8 Breathing

How it works: This method slows your heart rate and promotes relaxation, making it perfect before bed or during stressful moments.

Steps:

1. Breathe in through your nose for a count of four.
2. Hold for a count of seven.
3. Blow out slowly through your mouth for a count of eight.

Repeat for four to eight cycles. You may feel your body naturally relax as you extend the exhale.

Diaphragmatic (Belly) Breathing

How it works: This technique engages your diaphragm, helping to reduce stress by activating the parasympathetic nervous system.

Steps:

1. Get into a comfortable position.
2. Put a hand on your chest and the other on your belly.
3. Breathe deeply in through your nose, letting your belly and not your chest rise.
4. Blow out slowly through your mouth, letting your belly fall.

Practice for five to ten minutes, focusing on the rise and fall of your belly.

Alternate Nostril Breathing (Nadi Shodhana)

How it works: This yogic breathing practice balances energy and calms the mind.

Steps:

1. Sit comfortably and use your thumb to close your right nostril.
2. Inhale deeply through your left nostril.
3. Close your left nostril with your ring finger and release your thumb to open the right nostril.
4. Exhale through your right nostril, then inhale through it.
5. Close your right nostril again and exhale through your left nostril.

Continue alternating for one to three minutes, finishing with an exhale through the left nostril.

These breathwork techniques are about stress relief and reclaiming a sense of control in moments of overwhelm. Remember, your breath is your constant ally, always available to ground and center you. With practice, you'll find yourself returning to these techniques with confidence and ease.

Body Scan Meditation Script: Embracing Relaxation and Awareness

The body scan meditation is one of the foundational practices of MBSR. It's a gentle way to connect with your body, release tension, and build awareness of the present moment. Think of it as a mental check-in with every part of your body—an opportunity to slow down, listen, and let go.

Here's a step-by-step guided script to help you practice the body scan meditation (Kabat-Zinn, n.d.).

1. **Settle in:** Find a space where you are comfortable and won't be disturbed. Lie down on your back with your arms resting by your sides, or sit comfortably in a chair with your feet flat on the ground. Allow your body to relax and your eyes to close if that feels comfortable.

2. **Begin with breath awareness:** Take a few deep breaths, inhaling through your nose and exhaling slowly through your mouth. Allow your breath to settle into a natural rhythm. Notice the sensation of the air moving in and out of your body.

3. **Bring awareness to the body:** Gently shift your attention to the sensations in your body. Feel the connection between your body and the surface beneath you. Notice the points of contact and the weight of your body pressing into the floor or chair.

4. **Focus on the feet:** Bring your awareness to your feet. Notice any sensations—warmth, coolness, tingling, or even a lack of sensation. Without judgment, simply observe what's present. Take a moment to mentally thank your feet for supporting you throughout the day.

5. **Move up the legs:** Gradually move your focus upward, first to your ankles, then to your calves, knees, and thighs. Pause at each area, noticing any tension, pressure, or comfort. Imagine each muscle softening and releasing with each exhale.

6. **Scan the torso:** Bring your awareness to your lower back and abdomen. Notice how your belly rises and falls with each breath. Allow any tightness or tension to melt away. Move up to your chest and ribcage, noticing the rhythm of your breath and the sensations in this area.

7. **Shift to the arms:** Focus on your fingers, hands, wrists, and arms. Observe any sensations, from subtle vibrations to warmth or coolness. Imagine the muscles in your arms releasing and softening.

8. **Bring attention to the neck and shoulders:** These areas often hold tension. Notice any tightness, stiffness, or discomfort. With each exhale, visualize the tension melting away, leaving your shoulders and neck relaxed and at ease.

9. **Focus on the head and face:** Bring your awareness to your jaw, cheeks, and forehead. Notice if you're holding any tension here. Relax your jaw, soften your forehead, and allow your entire face to feel at ease.

10. **Feel the whole body:** Take a moment to expand your awareness to your entire body. Notice how it feels as a whole—connected, grounded, and relaxed. Breathe deeply, appreciating this moment of stillness and connection.

11. **Close the practice:** When you're ready, gently bring your attention back to your surroundings. Move your fingers and toes, and slowly open your eyes. Take a moment to notice how you feel—lighter, calmer, or more grounded.

The body scan meditation isn't about forcing relaxation or avoiding discomfort. It's about meeting your body where it is with curiosity and compassion. Over time, this practice can help you develop a deeper connection to yourself and a greater capacity for mindfulness in everyday life. Remember, each scan is a new opportunity to listen, let go, and simply be.

Loving-Kindness Meditation Script: Cultivating Compassion and Connection

Loving-kindness meditation, also known as *metta*, is a beautiful practice that nurtures compassion, kindness, and goodwill—

toward yourself, loved ones, and even people who challenge you. This meditation is about cultivating a heart full of love and sending it outward in ever-widening circles. It's like giving the world a warm hug, starting with yourself.

Here's a step-by-step script to guide you through a loving-kindness meditation practice (Kabat-Zinn, 2018):

- **Settle in:** Find a comfortable position, either sitting or lying down. Close your eyes or keep a soft gaze. Take a few deep breaths, inhaling through your nose and exhaling slowly through your mouth. Let your body relax and settle into the present moment.
- **Begin with yourself:** Bring your attention inward. Picture yourself in your mind's eye, or simply focus on the sensation of your own presence. Silently repeat these phrases to yourself:
  - May I be happy.
  - May I be healthy.
  - May I be safe.
  - May I live with ease.

Say these phrases slowly and intentionally, letting the meaning sink in. If you feel resistance or self-judgment, acknowledge it without judgment and continue the practice with kindness.

- **Expand to a loved one:** Bring to mind someone you deeply care about—someone who brings joy to your heart. Visualize them clearly or feel their presence. Silently repeat the phrases for them:
  - May you be happy.
  - May you be healthy.
  - May you be safe.

○ May you live with ease.

Imagine sending them warmth and love with each phrase, like a gentle light radiating from your heart to theirs.

- **Include a neutral person:** Next, think of someone neutral —perhaps a neighbor, coworker, or someone you see regularly but don't know well. Hold their image or presence in your mind. Repeat the phrases for them:
  ○ May you be happy.
  ○ May you be healthy.
  ○ May you be safe.
  ○ May you live with ease.

This step helps expand your circle of compassion beyond your immediate connections.

- **Extend to someone who challenges you:** Now, bring to mind someone with whom you've experienced difficulty or conflict. This can be challenging, so approach it gently. Visualize them, if possible, and repeat the phrases:
  ○ May you be happy.
  ○ May you be healthy.
  ○ May you be safe.
  ○ May you live with ease.

You don't have to excuse or condone their actions; this is about freeing yourself from anger or resentment and extending goodwill from a place of inner peace.

- **Encompass all beings:** Finally, expand your compassion to include all living beings—those near and far, those you know and those you'll never meet. Visualize your loving-

kindness radiating outward like ripples in a pond.
Repeat:
  ◦ May all beings be happy.
  ◦ May all beings be healthy.
  ◦ May all beings be safe.
  ◦ May all beings live with ease.
- **Close the practice:** Take a deep breath in and slowly exhale. Reflect on the sense of warmth and connection you've cultivated. Gently open your eyes and take a moment to return to your surroundings.

Loving-kindness meditation is a practice of the heart, and like any skill, it deepens with time and patience. It's okay if some steps feel harder than others; start where you are and let the practice grow. Over time, this meditation can help you foster more compassion, not only for others but for yourself. And who couldn't use a little more kindness in their day?

OBJECT CONCENTRATION MEDITATION SCRIPT: TRAINING YOUR MIND'S SPOTLIGHT

Concentration meditation is about focusing your attention on a single object, anchoring your mind to the present moment. This practice strengthens mental clarity, improves focus, and helps quiet the endless chatter in your head. The "object" can be anything—a candle flame, a sound, a visual image, or even a simple object like a pebble or your breath.

Here's a step-by-step script to guide you through an object/concentration meditation practice (Yoga, 2018).

1. **Choose your object of focus:** Select something simple and calming. It could be:

- A physical object, like a candle flame, a flower, or a pebble.
- A sound, such as a bell, white noise, or a mantra.
- A sensation, like your breath or the feeling of your hands resting in your lap.

2. **Settle in:** Find a comfortable and quiet place to sit. Rest your hands on your knees or in your lap, and allow your spine to be tall but relaxed. Close your eyes if you're focusing on a sound or sensation, or keep them softly open if your object is visual.

3. **Begin with grounding:** Take a few deep breaths, inhaling through your nose and exhaling through your mouth. Feel your body settling into stillness. Let go of distractions and bring your full attention to the present moment.

4. **Focus on the object:** Direct your attention to your chosen object. If it's visual, observe its details—the shape, texture, colors, or flickering light. If it's a sound, notice its tone, rhythm, and how it vibrates in your awareness. If it's your breath, feel the air moving in and out of your nostrils or the rise and fall of your chest.

5. **Redirect when distracted:** When your mind wanders (it will), gently notice where it went—no judgment. Acknowledge the thought, and then guide your focus back to your object. Imagine it like training a puppy: gently, patiently, and with kindness.

6. **Deepen the concentration:** As you maintain your focus, try to immerse yourself more fully in the experience. Notice subtleties you may have missed before—perhaps the flicker of the candle or the faint sound beneath your primary focus. Let your attention settle deeply into the object.

7. **Use an anchor if needed:** If your mind continues to wander, try using a silent word or phrase as a cue, such as

"focus" or "here." This can act as a mental nudge to bring your attention back.

8. **Close the practice:** After 10 minutes (or longer, if you'd like), gently release your focus on the object. Take a few deep breaths, and let your awareness expand to the room around you. Open your eyes if they were closed, and take a moment to notice how you feel—more calm, focused, or present.

Tips for Concentration Meditation

- **Start small:** Begin with five minutes and gradually increase the time as your focus improves.
- **Choose a Calming Object:** Pick something that naturally draws your attention without overstimulating it.
- **Be Patient:** It's normal for your mind to wander—think of every redirection as part of the practice.
- **Practice Regularly:** Consistency is key. Over time, you'll find it easier to maintain focus both during meditation and in daily life.

Concentration meditation is like a mental gym session, strengthening your mind's ability to stay present and focused. Over time, this practice can bring a sense of clarity and calm that carries over into your daily life. And remember, it's not about achieving perfection—it's about showing up, refocusing when needed, and enjoying the process of connecting deeply with the moment.

WALKING MEDITATION SCRIPT: FINDING PEACE IN EVERY STEP

Walking meditation is a beautiful way to bring mindfulness into motion. It combines the grounding benefits of walking with the awareness and focus of meditation, helping you connect with your body, your breath, and the world around you. It's perfect for moments when sitting still feels challenging or when you want to practice mindfulness in a more active way.

Here's a step-by-step script to guide you through a walking meditation practice (Sutton, 2020):

1. **Choose your path:** Find a quiet, safe space to walk. It can be indoors, like a hallway or room, or outdoors in a park, garden, or quiet street. Choose a path where you can walk back and forth or in a loop to avoid distractions like navigating traffic.
2. **Stand still to begin:** Start by standing still with your feet hip-width apart. Take a moment to feel your connection to the ground. Notice the sensations in your feet—the weight, pressure, or tingling. Let your body relax and settle into the present moment.
3. **Focus on your breath:** Take a few deep breaths, inhaling through your nose and exhaling through your mouth. Allow your breathing to find a natural rhythm. Notice how the air moves in and out, grounding you in this moment.
4. **Set an intention:** Before you start walking, set a simple intention for your practice. This might be to cultivate calm, focus, or gratitude. Hold this intention gently in your mind.
5. **Begin walking slowly:** Start walking at a slow, deliberate pace. Pay attention to the physical sensations of walking—the lifting of one foot, the movement through the air, and the placement of your foot back on the ground. Notice how your weight shifts from one foot to the other.

6. **Focus on each step:** With each step, silently say to yourself: This labeling helps anchor your attention to the act of walking.
   - "**Lifting**" as you lift your foot.
   - "**Moving**" as your foot moves forward.
   - "**Placing**" as your foot touches the ground.
7. **Coordinate with your breath:** Match your breath to your steps if it feels natural. For example:
   - Inhale over two steps: "Lift, move."
   - Exhale over the next two steps: "Place, shift."
8. **Engage all your senses:** As you walk, expand your awareness to the sights, sounds, and smells around you. Notice the texture of the ground beneath your feet, the temperature of the air, or the sounds of nature or your surroundings. Let yourself be fully present in the experience.
9. **Handle wandering thoughts:** If your mind wanders (and it will), gently acknowledge the distraction without judgment and bring your focus back to your steps or breath. Each time you return is part of the practice.
10. **Pause and reflect:** After a few minutes, stop walking and stand still. Take a deep breath and notice how your body feels. Reflect on any sense of calm, clarity, or connection that the practice has brought.
11. **Close the practice:** When you're ready to end your meditation, take a moment to thank yourself for practicing. If you're outdoors, appreciate the natural world around you. Walk back to your starting point at a natural pace, carrying the sense of mindfulness into the rest of your day.

Tips for Walking Meditation

- **Adjust your pace:** Go as slowly or as briskly as feels comfortable. The key is staying present, not sticking to a particular speed.
- **Practice anywhere:** While nature is ideal, you can also practice walking meditation in a hallway, office, or even while waiting in line.
- **Be kind to yourself:** If it feels awkward at first, that's okay! Like any skill, walking meditation becomes easier with practice.

Walking meditation is a reminder that mindfulness doesn't have to be still—it can move, flow, and evolve with you. With every step, you have the opportunity to ground yourself, clear mental clutter, and create a sense of peace. Whether it's a five-minute walk or a leisurely stroll through a park, each step is a chance to come back to yourself.

URGE SURFING: RIDING THE WAVE OF TEMPTATION

Urge surfing is a mindfulness-based technique that helps you manage cravings, impulses, or intense emotions without giving in to them. Think of an urge like a wave—it rises, peaks, and eventually subsides. Instead of resisting or fighting it, urge surfing teaches you to ride the wave with awareness and curiosity, allowing the urge to pass naturally.

This practice can be transformative for anyone dealing with cravings, whether it's for food, smoking, alcohol, social media, or even reacting impulsively to strong emotions like anger or frustration.

Urge Surfing Practice: Step-by-Step Guide

When you resist an urge, it often becomes stronger—like trying to push a beach ball underwater. Instead, urge surfing invites you to observe the urge without judgment, accepting it as it is. By doing so, you're retraining your brain to respond calmly and thoughtfully rather than reactively (Sutton, 2024).

1. **Pause and recognize the urge:** When you notice a craving or impulse arising, pause. Acknowledge its presence by silently saying to yourself, "I feel an urge to [describe the craving or impulse]." Avoid judging it—just observe.

2. **Focus on your breath:** Take a few deep breaths to ground yourself. Feel the air moving in and out of your body. This helps create a moment of mindfulness, separating you from the automatic reaction to the urge.

3. **Observe the urge:** Imagine the urge as a wave. Notice how it feels in your body—where do you feel it most strongly? Maybe it's a tightness in your chest, a flutter in your stomach, or a tingling in your hands. Simply observe these sensations with curiosity, as though you're a scientist studying them.

4. **Describe the sensations:** Mentally note what you're feeling. For example: Observing and describing your sensations can help you detach from the urge and see it for what it is—temporary sensations in your body.
   - "I feel a warmth in my chest."
   - "There's tension in my jaw."
   - "My hands feel restless."

5. **Ride the wave:** As you continue to observe the urge, imagine yourself riding it like a surfer on a wave. Notice how it changes—it might grow stronger, but eventually, it

will begin to fade. Remind yourself that all urges, no matter how intense, are temporary.

6. **Let it pass:** With time, the wave of the urge will naturally subside. Stay present with your breath and body as it fades. Acknowledge the effort you've put into staying mindful and congratulate yourself for not reacting impulsively.

7. **Redirect your focus:** Once the urge has passed, gently shift your attention to something else—perhaps your surroundings, a calming activity, or your breath. This reinforces your ability to move on without giving in to the craving.

Tips for Practicing Urge Surfing

- **Start small:** Practice with mild urges before tackling more intense ones. This helps you build confidence in your ability to handle them.
- **Be kind to yourself:** If you give in to an urge, don't beat yourself up. Recognize it as part of the learning process and try again next time.
- **Use a timer:** If it's helpful, set a timer for 10 minutes and commit to urge surfing for that duration. Often, urges will pass within that time.
- **Practice regularly:** Like any skill, urge surfing gets easier with practice. Over time, you'll notice urges have less power over you.

Urge surfing is rooted in mindfulness and the idea of acceptance. Research shows that observing and accepting cravings without judgment can reduce their intensity and frequency over time. By not engaging in the cycle of resistance or indulgence, you weaken the brain's habitual response to cravings, fostering greater emotional resilience and self-control (Sutton, 2024).

Urges don't have to control you—they're simply waves you can learn to ride. Through urge surfing, you can develop the strength to face cravings and impulses with calm and curiosity, allowing them to pass without giving in. Remember, each time you ride the wave successfully, you're building the foundation for greater emotional freedom and self-mastery.

MINDFUL STRETCHING: CONNECTING MOVEMENT AND AWARENESS

Mindful stretching is a practice that combines gentle physical movements with focused awareness, creating a bridge between your body and mind. It's not about achieving the deepest stretch or perfect posture—it's about being present with your body as it moves and feels, noticing sensations, and honoring your limits with kindness.

This practice is a great way to reduce tension, increase flexibility, and cultivate mindfulness, whether you're starting your day, taking a break, or winding down (Visvanathan, 2024).

Mindful Stretching Practice: Step-by-Step Guide

1. **Prepare your space:** Choose a quiet, comfortable space where you can stretch without distractions. Wear loose, comfortable clothing that allows free movement. If needed, use a yoga mat or soft surface for support.
2. **Begin with breath awareness:** Stand or sit tall. Close your eyes if you are comfortable doing so. Take a few deep breaths, inhaling through your nose and exhaling through your mouth. Let your body settle into stillness and your mind into the present moment.

3. **Neck stretch:**
   - Inhale as you lengthen your spine.
   - On the exhale, gently tilt your head to one side, bringing your ear toward your shoulder. Feel the stretch along the opposite side of your neck.
   - Hold for a few breaths, noticing any sensations.
   - Inhale as you return to center, then exhale to stretch the other side.

4. **Shoulder roll:**
   - Inhale as you lift your shoulders toward your ears.
   - Exhale as you roll them back and down, feeling the release.
   - Repeat 3–5 times, moving slowly and with awareness.

5. **Seated forward fold:**
   - Sit on the floor with your legs extended in front of you.
   - Inhale to lengthen your spine, and exhale as you gently hinge forward at the hips.
   - Let your hands rest on your legs, ankles, or feet—wherever feels comfortable.
   - Hold the stretch for 5–10 breaths, noticing sensations in your hamstrings and lower back.

6. **Cat-cow stretch:**
   - Come to a tabletop position on your hands and knees.
   - Inhale as you arch your back, lifting your head and tailbone (Cow Pose).
   - Exhale as you round your spine, tucking your chin and tailbone (Cat Pose).
   - Move through these poses slowly, syncing your breath with each movement. Repeat for 5–10 breaths.

7. **Side stretch:**
   - Stand or sit with your feet hip-width apart.
   - Inhale as you reach one arm overhead.

- Exhale as you gently lean to the opposite side, creating a stretch along your side body.
- Hold for a few breaths, then repeat on the other side.

8. **Final resting pose:**
   - Lie on your back with your arms by your sides and your palms facing up.
   - Close your eyes and let your body relax completely.
   - Take 10 deep breaths, feeling the effects of your practice.

Mindfulness Tips for Stretching

- **Move slowly:** Focus on the sensations in your body as you stretch. Avoid rushing or forcing any movement.
- **Stay curious:** Notice how each stretch feels. Where do you feel tension or ease? Let go of judgment and simply observe.
- **Sync with your breath:** Use your inhale to lengthen and expand and your exhale to release and deepen the stretch.
- **Honor your limits:** Stretch to a point of gentle discomfort, not pain. Respect your body's boundaries and let them guide you.

WHEN TO PRACTICE MINDFUL STRETCHING

- **Morning wake-up:** Loosen up stiffness and start your day with calm energy.
- **Workday break:** Release tension from sitting at a desk or working on a screen.
- **Evening wind-down:** Relax your body and mind before bed for better sleep.

Mindful stretching is more than just physical movement—it's a way to build a compassionate connection with your body. As you stretch, let go of any need to "achieve" something and instead focus on the act of being present. With every stretch, breath, and moment, you're honoring your body and inviting mindfulness into your life.

MINDFUL EATING: NOURISHING YOUR BODY AND SOUL

Mindful eating is about changing the way you experience food. It's not a diet, a set of rules, or a quick fix—it's an invitation to slow down, savor every bite, and connect with your body's needs. When you eat mindfully, you create a healthier relationship with food, reduce overeating, and enjoy your meals with greater satisfaction.

Mindful eating is the practice of bringing full awareness to your eating experience. It involves noticing the colors, textures, smells, and tastes of your food while tuning in to your body's hunger and fullness signals. It's about eating with intention and attention rather than mindlessly munching while scrolling on your phone or rushing through meals (Bjarnadottir, 2023).

Mindful Eating Practice: Step-by-Step Guide

1. **Create a calm eating environment:** Choose a quiet, distraction-free space to eat. Turn off the TV, put your phone away, and sit down at a table. Set the scene for a peaceful meal.
2. **Take a moment of gratitude:** Before you begin eating, take a moment to appreciate your meal. Reflect on the effort that went into growing, preparing, and serving the

food in front of you. A brief pause can set a mindful tone for your meal.

3. **Engage your senses:** Observe your food with curiosity. Notice the colors, shapes, and textures. Smell the aroma and take in the presentation. As you take your first bite, pay attention to the flavors, temperature, and how the food feels in your mouth.

4. **Chew slowly and fully:** Chew each bite thoroughly, noticing how the flavors evolve. Eating slowly not only helps with digestion but also gives your brain time to register fullness.

5. **Tune into hunger and fullness cues:** Pause periodically during your meal to ask yourself how hungry or full you feel. Use a scale of one to ten, with one being starving and ten being overly full. Aim to stop eating when you feel comfortably satisfied, around a six or seven.

6. **Notice your thoughts and emotions:** Pay attention to any thoughts or feelings that arise as you eat. Are you genuinely hungry, or are you eating out of boredom, stress, or habit? Approach these observations with curiosity, not judgment.

7. **Savor each bite:** Treat each bite as an opportunity to fully experience your food. Avoid rushing to the next bite—let the flavors and textures linger.

8. **End with gratitude:** When you finish eating, take a moment to express gratitude for the nourishment your meal provided. Notice how your body feels—energized, satisfied, or relaxed.

The Benefits of Mindful Eating

- **Improves digestion:** Eating slowly and chewing thoroughly helps your body digest food more efficiently.

- **Reduces overeating:** Tuning in to hunger and fullness cues helps prevent overeating and encourages portion control.
- **Enhances enjoyment:** Fully engaging your senses makes meals more satisfying and pleasurable.
- **Supports emotional awareness:** Recognizing emotional eating patterns allows you to address them without judgment.
- **Promotes healthy habits:** Mindful eating builds a deeper connection with food, encouraging more thoughtful choices.

Tips for Practicing Mindful Eating

- **Start small:** Begin with one mindful meal or snack a day. Build the habit gradually.
- **Put down your fork:** Between bites, put your fork down and take a breath. This prevents rushing through your meal.
- **Avoid multitasking:** Make eating the main event—no screens, work, or distractions.
- **Be kind to yourself:** If you slip into old habits, don't worry. Gently guide yourself back to mindfulness.

Mindful Eating Exercise: The Raisin Experiment

This classic mindfulness exercise helps you slow down and truly experience food. Here's how to try it (Bjarnadottir, 2023):

1. Take a single raisin and hold it in your hand.
2. Observe it closely—notice its shape, texture, color, and any other details.
3. Smell the raisin and note its aroma.

4. Place it in your mouth, but don't chew yet. Feel its texture with your tongue.
5. Chew slowly, noticing the flavors as they unfold.
6. Swallow and take a moment to reflect on the experience.

Mindful eating is a practice of awareness, patience, and self-compassion. It's not about restriction or guilt—it's about honoring your body and the food that nourishes it. With time, mindful eating can transform your meals into moments of connection, gratitude, and joy. So, the next time you sit down to eat, let mindfulness be your secret ingredient.

Mindfulness isn't just something you practice on a mat or cushion —it's a way of living. Whether you're savoring a meal, taking a mindful walk, or pausing to breathe through a moment of stress, each small act of awareness strengthens your connection to the present. When you incorporate these techniques into your daily life, you create space for clarity, calm, and compassion to flourish.

As we close this chapter, remember: mindfulness is a process, a way of life. Every breath, every step, every bite can be a reminder to slow down and be here now.

In the next chapter, we'll take this foundation of awareness and explore the second modality: Dialectical Behavior Therapy (DBT) —a powerful approach to navigating emotions, building resilience, and creating meaningful connections. Let's keep moving forward together!

MODALITY TWO

DIALECTICAL BEHAVIOR THERAPY (DBT)

CHAPTER 4: EMOTIONAL FIRST AID KIT

ESSENTIAL DBT SKILLS FOR SELF-COMPASSION

 Pain is inevitable. Suffering is optional.

— *HARUKI MURAKAMI*

Let's talk about those days when your emotions feel like a hurricane—everything swirling, chaotic, and completely out of control. You know the ones I'm talking about: when the smallest inconvenience sends you spiraling or when you feel so overwhelmed that even deciding what's for dinner feels like climbing the biggest mountain. Been there, done that, right? That's why I want to introduce you to what I like to call your emotional first aid kit, packed with skills from dialectical behavior therapy (DBT).

Now, I know therapy might sound clinical or even intimidating, but DBT is the cool, approachable friend you didn't know you needed. It's practical, down-to-earth, and ridiculously effective when it comes to handling those big, messy emotions. Think of it as the Swiss Army knife of emotional regulation—whether you're battling anxiety, self-doubt, or just the nagging voice in your head that says you're not enough, DBT has got your back.

This chapter is all about teaching you essential DBT skills to handle emotional challenges with confidence, grace, and self-compassion. We're diving into the nitty-gritty of self-soothing, mindfulness, and boundary-setting—not as abstract ideas but as tools you can actually use in real life. I'm talking about strategies that work when your boss criticizes your work, your best friend cancels plans last minute, or you're stuck in traffic with a playlist full of songs that hit a little too close to home. How does Adele always know, right?

By the end of this chapter, you'll have your very own emotional first aid kit, complete with skills that empower you to face life's challenges with courage and self-compassion.

DEMYSTIFYING DBT: WHAT IT IS, WHO IT HELPS, AND WHY IT WORKS

Before we dive into how DBT can change your emotional world, let's take a moment to demystify what it actually is. The name might sound a little complicated—*Dialectical Behavior Therapy*—but don't let it intimidate you. At its heart, DBT is a practical and effective approach to managing emotions, building healthier relationships, and creating a life that feels more balanced and fulfilling.

Developed by Dr. Marsha Linehan, DBT was initially designed to help people with intense emotional challenges, particularly those diagnosed with borderline personality disorder (BPD) (Schimelpfening, 2023). However, over time, it became clear that the skills DBT teaches—mindfulness, emotional regulation, distress tolerance, and interpersonal effectiveness—can benefit anyone who struggles with emotional ups and downs.

At its core, DBT is rooted in the idea of dialectics, which is a fancy way of saying it's all about balancing opposites. For instance, DBT teaches you how to accept yourself as you are right now while working to change behaviors or patterns that don't serve you. It's about finding the sweet spot between acceptance and growth—a compassionate middle ground where both can coexist (Schimelpfening, 2023).

DBT is a powerhouse for emotional healing and resilience. Here's what makes it so effective:

- **Emotional freedom:** It helps you identify and regulate intense emotions so they no longer control your actions or cloud your thinking.
- **Crisis management:** DBT gives you tools to handle emotional crises without resorting to self-destructive behaviors or unhealthy coping mechanisms.
- **Improved relationships:** Through interpersonal effectiveness skills, you learn how to set boundaries, communicate clearly, and manage conflict with confidence and respect.
- **Mindfulness mastery:** DBT teaches you to stay present in the moment, reducing anxiety about the future and regrets about the past.

Whether you're dealing with anxiety, depression, emotional over-whelm, or just the stress of everyday life, DBT offers something for everyone.

The Four Dysregulations of DBT

At its heart, DBT is designed to address four key areas where people often feel out of balance, known as the four dysregulations. Understanding these can help you identify where you might benefit the most from DBT:

1. **Emotional dysregulation:** This refers to the inability to manage intense emotions effectively. If you've ever felt like your emotions are a runaway train, this one's for you.
2. **Behavioral dysregulation:** When emotions feel out of control, behaviors often follow suit. DBT helps you replace impulsive or destructive reactions with healthier, more deliberate choices.
3. **Cognitive dysregulation:** Ever find yourself trapped in negative thought spirals or black-and-white thinking? DBT addresses this by teaching you to challenge unhelpful thoughts and embrace more balanced perspectives.
4. **Interpersonal dysregulation:** Struggles with maintaining healthy relationships, setting boundaries, or resolving conflicts fall under this category. DBT equips you with skills to build stronger, more fulfilling connections.

The Four Stages of DBT

To help people systematically work through these challenges, DBT is structured into four stages. Each stage builds on the one before it, creating a step-by-step path to emotional freedom and resilience.

1. **Stabilization:** The first stage focuses on helping you gain control of destructive behaviors and emotional crises. This is where distress tolerance and mindfulness skills come into play.
2. **Exploration:** Once you've achieved stability, the second stage is about exploring the root causes of your emotional pain, such as past trauma or unresolved issues.
3. **Skill building:** At this stage, the focus shifts to strengthening your emotional and interpersonal skills. You'll learn how to live with more balance, mindfulness, and self-compassion.
4. **Empowerment:** The final stage is about creating a life worth living—a life that aligns with your values, passions, and purpose. This stage is all about growing, not just getting by.

Who Can DBT Help?

While DBT was originally developed for those with BPD, its applications go far beyond that. DBT is now widely used to support people facing challenges such as (Schimelpfening, 2023):

- anxiety and depression
- PTSD and trauma
- eating disorders
- substance use disorders
- emotional overwhelm and stress
- chronic conflict in relationships

Whether you identify with any of these or just feel like your emotions occasionally get the best of you, DBT has something to offer.

Before we get to the techniques, take a moment to reflect: Which of these four dysregulations resonates most with you? Identifying your emotional pain points is the first step in transforming them into strengths.

TECHNIQUES OF DBT: YOUR EMOTIONAL TOOLKIT

Now that we've laid the groundwork for understanding DBT, it's time to open up your emotional first aid kit and dive into the techniques that make DBT so transformative. These aren't abstract concepts—they're practical, actionable tools you can use to handle emotional storms with resilience, grace, and self-compassion. Let's explore the big ones: distress tolerance, self-soothing techniques, grounding techniques, and the life-changing practice of radical acceptance.

Distress Tolerance: Riding Out the Storm

Life is messy, period. Distress tolerance skills are all about helping you survive those overwhelming moments without making the situation worse. When emotions feel unbearable, these techniques offer a lifeline, helping you stay grounded and clear-headed until the storm passes.

Key strategies include the following.

TIPP (Temperature, Intense Exercise, Paced Breathing, Progressive Relaxation)

When emotions are at their peak—whether it's anxiety, anger, or overwhelm—it can feel like your body is in overdrive, hijacked by stress. This is where TIPP comes in: a set of scientifically backed techniques that help bring your nervous system back to baseline (*DBT : TIPP - Skills, Worksheets, Videos, & Activities*, 2024). The acronym stands for temperature, intense exercise, paced breathing, and progressive relaxation—four powerhouse strategies that are simple to use and remarkably effective. Let's unpack how each one works and how you can use them in your daily life.

Temperature: Cool Down to Calm Down

When emotions are running hot, literally cooling down your body can have an immediate calming effect. This works because sudden cold exposure activates your body's dive reflex, slowing your heart rate and calming your nervous system.

How to use it:

- Splash cold water on your face or run your wrists under cold water for 30 seconds.
- Hold an ice pack or frozen peas against your face, particularly on your cheeks and under your eyes.
- Dip your face in a bowl of cold water for a few seconds at a time (yes, it works!).

The cold sensation signals your brain to shift from a state of fight-or-flight to a calmer, more regulated state. It's like hitting the reset button for your body.

Intense Exercise: Move to Burn Off Stress

When emotions feel overwhelming, intense exercise can help discharge the energy fueling your stress. Think of it as using up the adrenaline surge your body creates when it's in a heightened emotional state.

How to use it:

- Do 30 seconds to 2 minutes of high-intensity exercise, like sprinting, jumping jacks, or running in place.

- Hit the ground with a set of push-ups, burpees, or mountain climbers.
- Go for a quick walk or run, even if it's just around the block.

Physical activity releases feel-good endorphins and metabolizes the stress hormones flooding your system, helping you feel more grounded and less overwhelmed (*DBT : TIPP - Skills, Worksheets, Videos, & Activities*, 2024).

Paced Breathing: Slow and Steady Wins the Calm

Your breath is one of the most powerful tools for calming your nervous system. When you're overwhelmed, breathing tends to become shallow and fast, which sends signals to your brain that you're in danger. By slowing your breath, you can convince your body that it's safe to relax (*DBT : TIPP - Skills, Worksheets, Videos, & Activities*, 2024).

How to use it:

- Try the 4-7-8 technique: Inhale for 4 seconds, hold for 7 seconds and exhale for 8 seconds. Repeat this cycle 4–5 times.
- Use box breathing: Inhale for 4 seconds, hold for 4 seconds, exhale for 4 seconds, and hold again for 4 seconds before starting the next breath.
- Focus on making your exhale longer than your inhale, which activates the calming parasympathetic nervous system.

Paced breathing reduces your heart rate and lowers cortisol levels, helping your mind and body return to a state of balance (Ma et al., 2017).

Progressive Relaxation: Release Tension, One Muscle at a Time

When you're stressed or upset, tension builds up in your body, often without you even realizing it. Progressive relaxation helps you let go of this physical tension by focusing on one muscle group at a time.

How to use it:

1. Find a comfortable seated or lying position.
2. Starting at your feet, tense your muscles as tightly as you can for five seconds, then release them completely.
3. Move upward through your body—calves, thighs, stomach, chest, arms, shoulders, neck—tensing and relaxing each muscle group as you go.
4. Finish by taking a few deep, calming breaths, and notice how much lighter your body feels.

Releasing physical tension signals your brain to let go of emotional stress as well, creating a powerful mind-body connection that fosters relaxation (Scott, 2024).

The beauty of TIPP is its flexibility—you don't have to use all four techniques every time. Instead, think of them as tools in a toolkit. If you're feeling panicked, start with temperature to quickly calm your body. If you're restless or agitated, try intense exercise to burn off the excess energy. For moments of quiet overwhelm, paced breathing, or progressive relaxation can help bring you back to center.

Practice these techniques regularly, even during calm moments, so they feel natural and accessible when you need them most. Over time, TIPP becomes not just an emergency response but a reliable way to build emotional resilience. You've got the tools—now it's time to use them to reclaim your calm.

Distract With Wise Mind ACCEPTS

When your emotions feel like a runaway train, Distract with Wise Mind ACCEPTS can help you hit the brakes. This acronym offers a variety of distraction strategies designed to shift your focus away from overwhelming emotions and onto constructive alternatives. It's not about avoiding your feelings but giving yourself the space to cool down so you can address them with clarity and intention.

Here's how to use ACCEPTS as your emotional toolkit (*Distract with Wise Mind ACCEPTS*, 2024):

Activities

Engage in something that occupies your mind and body, giving your emotions a chance to settle. Activities don't have to be grand or time-consuming; even small, enjoyable tasks can work wonders.

Examples:

- Read a book, watch a favorite movie, or listen to a podcast.
- Go for a walk, bake something, or organize a cluttered drawer.
- Start a hobby you love, like painting, knitting, or playing an instrument.

Focusing on an activity redirects your attention, giving your brain a break from ruminating or catastrophizing (Cirino, 2024).

Contributing

Sometimes, helping others can be the best way to help yourself. Acts of kindness shift your focus outward and can boost your sense of purpose and connection.

Examples:

- Volunteer at a local charity or food bank.
- Help a friend or family member with a task they're struggling with.
- Send an encouraging text to someone who needs it.

Contributing to others creates positive emotions, enhancing your mood and helping you see beyond your immediate stress.

Comparisons

Shift your perspective by comparing your current situation to one that's less distressing or even more challenging. This isn't about minimizing your feelings but about gaining a broader view of your circumstances.

Examples:

- Reflect on a time when you overcame a similar challenge and remind yourself of your resilience.
- Think about someone you admire who has faced similar struggles and how they coped.

Comparisons can provide perspective and remind you of your strength and ability to overcome difficulties.

Emotions

Engage in something that sparks a different emotional reaction. This strategy is about disrupting the intensity of your current emotion by introducing a contrasting feeling.

Examples:

- Watch a funny video or read something uplifting.
- Listen to a song that inspires or energizes you.
- Revisit happy memories by looking through old photos.

Replacing a negative emotional state with a positive or neutral one can create space for calm and clarity.

Pushing Away

When emotions are overwhelming, sometimes the best strategy is to mentally set them aside for a moment. This doesn't mean ignoring them forever, but temporarily parking them to give yourself a breather.

Examples:

- Visualize placing your distress in a box and setting it on a shelf.
- Write your thoughts down and promise yourself you'll revisit them later.

Temporarily pushing away emotions helps you regain control, so they don't dominate your actions.

Thoughts

Distracting your mind with neutral or unrelated thoughts can break the cycle of overwhelming emotions. It's like changing the channel when the current one feels too intense.

Examples:

- Count backward from 100 by sevens.
- Recite a poem, quote, or song lyrics in your head.

- Solve a brainteaser or do a quick crossword puzzle.

Engaging your logical brain gives your emotional brain a chance to calm down (Holland, 2023).

Sensations

Focusing on physical sensations grounds you in the present moment and helps redirect your energy.

Examples:

- Hold a comforting object, like a soft blanket or stress ball.
- Take a hot shower or splash cold water on your face.
- Chew mint gum or suck on a sour candy to engage your taste buds.

Sensory input brings your attention back to your body, anchoring you in the here and now (Kuyken, 2024).

When you're overwhelmed, the urge to act impulsively—whether it's sending an angry text, overeating, or indulging in another unhealthy behavior—can feel irresistible. This is where weighing pros and cons becomes a lifesaver. It slows down your decision-making process and helps you align your actions with your long-term goals.

How to Use Pros and Cons

- **Write it down:** Divide a sheet of paper into two columns —pros and cons.
- **Consider the urge:** List the short and long-term benefits and drawbacks of acting on your impulse.
  - Pros: "It might feel good to vent my anger right now."

- ○ Cons: "It could damage the relationship and make me feel worse later."
- **Think of alternatives:** Add a third column if needed to weigh the pros and cons of alternative actions. For example, "Take a walk instead of sending the text."
- **Pause and reflect:** Review your list and take a deep breath before deciding.

This process activates the rational part of your brain, overriding the emotional, impulsive response. It also helps you see the bigger picture, making it easier to choose actions that align with your values and long-term happiness.

Both Wise Mind ACCEPTS and pros and cons are about creating space between your emotions and your actions. They empower you to choose responses that serve you instead of reactions that derail you. The next time you feel like your emotions are about to take over, remember these tools—they're your keys to regaining control, one thoughtful choice at a time.

Self-Soothing Techniques: Comforting Yourself Like a Pro

When you're feeling emotionally raw, self-soothing techniques come to the rescue. These skills help you nurture yourself by engaging your senses—touch, sight, sound, taste, and smell—to create a sense of calm and safety.

Here's how to build your self-soothing arsenal:

- **Touch:** Wrap yourself in a cozy blanket, pet a soft animal, or take a warm bath. Physical comfort can be incredibly grounding.

- **Sight:** Look at calming visuals, like photos of loved ones, nature scenes, or your favorite artwork. Better yet, step outside and let nature work its magic.
- **Sound:** Create a playlist of songs that calm or uplift you or tune into soothing sounds like rain, waves, or birdsong.
- **Taste:** Savor a comforting drink or treat—a warm cup of tea or a square of dark chocolate can work wonders.
- **Smell:** Light a candle, diffuse essential oils, or simply take in the scent of fresh flowers.

Think of self-soothing as a hug for your soul—sometimes, a little sensory comfort is all you need to reset.

Grounding Techniques: Finding Your Anchor

When emotions feel overwhelming, grounding techniques pull you back to the present moment. They're especially useful for managing anxiety, panic, or dissociation.

Here are some go-to grounding strategies:

- **5-4-3-2-1 technique:** Identify five things you see, four things you feel, three things you hear, two things you smell, and one thing you taste. This simple exercise shifts your focus away from distress and onto your immediate environment (Gupta, 2024).
- **Breath awareness:** Focus on the rhythm of your breathing. Inhale deeply for a count of four, hold for four, and exhale for four. Repeat until you feel calmer.
- **Physical grounding:** Press your feet firmly into the ground, grip a sturdy object, or splash cold water on your face. The physical sensation helps you reconnect with the present.

Grounding techniques are like mental anchors—they keep you steady when emotional waves threaten to sweep you away.

Radical Acceptance: The Game-Changer

If there's one DBT skill that can change your relationship with life, it's radical acceptance. This technique isn't about giving up or condoning painful situations—it's about acknowledging reality as it is, without judgment, resistance, or denial. It's the key to freeing yourself from emotional suffering caused by fighting against what you can't change.

Here's how to practice radical acceptance (Cuncic, 2024):

- **Acknowledge the present moment:** Start by recognizing the reality of your situation. For example, instead of resisting the fact that it's raining, simply note, "It's raining."
- **Let go of "shoulds" and "if onlys":** Replace thoughts like, "This shouldn't have happened," with, "This is where I am right now."
- **Use self-talk:** Remind yourself, "I can't change the past, but I can choose how I respond moving forward."
- **Turn the mind:** When you notice yourself resisting reality, gently guide your mind back to acceptance. It's a skill you'll strengthen over time.

Radical acceptance doesn't mean you stop striving for change—it means you stop wasting energy fighting against reality, freeing yourself to move forward with clarity and strength.

EMOTIONAL REGULATION: MASTERING YOUR INNER WORLD

Emotions can be complicated. One moment, you're fine, and the next, a wave of anger, sadness, or anxiety can hit you like a ton of bricks. Sound familiar? If so, you're not alone. Emotions are part of being human, but they don't have to control your life. Emotional regulation is all about understanding your emotions, handling them with confidence, and learning how to respond in ways that align with your values and goals.

Think of it as becoming the captain of your emotional ship—no matter how choppy the waters get, you're the one steering. Let's dive into how to master emotional regulation with grace, strength, and, yes, a dash of self-compassion.

Understanding Your Emotions: Your Built-In GPS

Emotions aren't random. They're your internal GPS, guiding you through life and helping you make sense of your experiences. Joy tells you when something feels right, anger signals that a boundary has been crossed, and sadness reminds you of what you value. Even anxiety has a purpose—it's your brain's way of keeping you alert to potential challenges.

But emotions are messengers, not dictators. They're meant to inform your actions, not control them. To regulate your emotions, you need to start by listening to them without letting them run the show, but how? Try the following:

- **Name it to tame it:** When you feel a strong emotion, pause and label it. Is it frustration? Guilt? Jealousy? Sometimes, just naming what you feel can help you calm down and gain clarity.

- **Ask what it's trying to tell you:** Emotions often carry valuable information. If you're angry, ask yourself, "What boundary might have been crossed?" If you're anxious, consider, "What am I afraid of, and is it realistic?"
- **Check the facts:** Emotions are powerful, but they're not always accurate. Take a step back and ask, "Is this emotion based on the situation in front of me, or am I reacting to something deeper?"

When you understand your emotions, you take the first step toward regulating them—because how can you steer the ship if you don't know where you're headed?

On Anger Management: Taming the Fire Without Losing the Spark

Let's talk about anger. It's often labeled as a "bad" emotion, but in reality, anger is neither good nor bad—it's just a signal that something feels wrong. The problem isn't anger itself; it's how we manage it. When left unchecked, anger can erupt like a volcano, leaving destruction in its wake. But when channeled effectively, it can become a powerful force for setting boundaries and advocating for yourself. So, how can we manage it? Give these a try:

- **Pause before you react:** When you feel anger bubbling up, pause. Take a deep breath and give yourself a moment to process before responding. This can prevent knee-jerk reactions you might regret later.
- **Channel it constructively:** Use your anger as motivation to address the issue. Write down what's bothering you and how you can approach it calmly and effectively.
- **Release it safely:** Anger is energy, and it needs an outlet. Try physical activities like going for a run, hitting a

punching bag, or even screaming into a pillow (yes, it works).

- **Communicate clearly:** When you're ready to address the issue, use "I" statements to express how you feel without blaming others. For example, "I felt hurt when you didn't include me" is more effective than "You never care about me."

Anger doesn't have to be a wildfire—it can be a controlled burn that clears the way for growth.

On Working Through Emotional Blocks: Breaking Free

Emotional blocks are those sticky, stubborn feelings that seem to hold you back no matter how hard you try. Maybe it's lingering guilt, fear of failure, or the weight of past experiences. Whatever it is, emotional blocks can feel like invisible chains—but the good news is, you hold the key to breaking free. Try the following to work through those emotional blocks:

- **Identify the block:** Ask yourself, "What's holding me back right now?" Be honest. Sometimes it's fear of rejection; other times, it's the voice of an old belief telling you you're not good enough.
- **Challenge the block:** Once you've identified the block, question its validity. Ask, "Is this belief true, or is it something I've been carrying unnecessarily?" Often, emotional blocks are based on stories we tell ourselves, not facts.
- **Use self-compassion:** Talk to yourself like you would a close friend. Instead of beating yourself up, say, "It's okay to feel this way, but I'm ready to move forward."

- **Take small steps:** Emotional blocks often feel overwhelming because they seem too big to tackle. Break them down into manageable steps. For example, if fear of failure is holding you back from pursuing a dream, start by setting one small, achievable goal.
- **Seek support:** Sometimes, working through emotional blocks requires an outside perspective. Don't hesitate to lean on a trusted friend, coach, or therapist for guidance.

Breaking through emotional blocks isn't about being fearless—it's about taking action even when fear is present. And every small step you take is a victory worth celebrating.

Regulating your emotions doesn't mean you'll never feel overwhelmed or upset—it means you'll know how to handle those feelings when they come. Remember, emotions are part of life, but they don't define you.

INTERPERSONAL EFFECTIVENESS: MASTERING THE ART OF BOUNDARIES

Let's talk about boundaries—the invisible lines that keep your relationships healthy, balanced, and mutually respectful. Whether you're setting boundaries, enforcing them, or respecting someone else's, boundaries are an essential part of maintaining emotional freedom, confidence, and self-compassion. They're not about shutting people out—they're about honoring your needs and creating space for healthier, more fulfilling connections.

So, if the idea of setting boundaries makes you feel awkward or unsure, don't worry. I'm here to help you find a clear understanding of what boundaries are, how to figure out your limits, and how to protect them while respecting others' needs, too.

Boundaries are the limits you set to define what's acceptable and unacceptable in your relationships, time, and energy. They're the rules of engagement for how others treat you—and how you treat yourself.

Think of boundaries as a personal fence:

- Inside the fence is what you value, protect, and allow to flourish (your needs, emotions, time, and energy).
- Outside the fence is what you decide doesn't serve or support you.

Boundaries are guidelines you establish to maintain your well-being, ensure respectful interactions, and create clarity in relationships (Hutchinson, n.d.).

Types of Boundaries

Boundaries come in all shapes and sizes, depending on what part of your life they protect. Here are some key types (Hutchinson, n.d.):

- **Physical boundaries:** These involve your personal space and physical touch.
  - Example: "I'm not comfortable hugging people I don't know well."
- **Emotional boundaries:** These protect your feelings and emotional energy.
  - Example: "I can't be the person you vent to every day—I need to take care of my own mental health."
- **Time boundaries:** These ensure your time is respected and valued.

- Example: "I need to log off by 6:00 p.m. to spend time with my family."
- **Intellectual boundaries:** These involve your thoughts, opinions, and ideas.
    - Example: "I prefer not to discuss politics during family dinners."
- **Material boundaries:** These relate to your possessions and finances.
    - Example: "I'm happy to lend you this, but I need it back by Friday."
- **Sexual boundaries:** These protect your comfort and consent in intimate situations.
    - Example: "I'm not ready for this step in our relationship."

Hard vs. Soft Boundaries

Boundaries can be flexible or firm, depending on the situation and your comfort level.

- **Hard boundaries:** These are non-negotiable limits you set to protect your well-being.
    - Example: "I don't tolerate yelling or name-calling in conversations."
- **Soft boundaries:** These are more flexible and may change depending on context or relationships.
    - Example: "I usually don't work on weekends, but I can make an exception for this project."

Both hard and soft boundaries are valuable—it's about knowing which to use and when.

Healthy vs. Unhealthy Boundaries

Boundaries should empower you, not isolate you. Here's how to spot the difference:

- **Healthy boundaries:**
  - You communicate your needs clearly and respectfully.
  - You take responsibility for your emotions and expect the same from others.
  - You feel safe, respected, and valued in your relationships.
- **Unhealthy boundaries:**
  - You avoid setting boundaries for fear of conflict or rejection.
  - You overextend yourself to please others.
  - You feel resentful, drained, or taken advantage of.

Feeling like a doormat? Constantly overwhelmed? These are red flags that you need stronger boundaries:

- You say yes when you really want to say no.
- You feel responsible for fixing other people's problems.
- You're frequently exhausted from overcommitting.
- You resent how others treat you but avoid speaking up.

If any of these hit close to home, it's time to start setting boundaries that prioritize your well-being.

Figuring Out Your Boundaries and Your Non-Negotiables

Before you can enforce boundaries, you need to know what they are. Here's how to get clear on your limits:

First, you need to identify your needs and values. Ask yourself:

- What drains my energy or makes me feel resentful?
- What activities, behaviors, or relationships feel nourishing?
- What do I need to feel safe, respected, and valued?

Next, you need to reflect on past experiences. Think about situations where you felt uncomfortable or taken advantage of. What could have prevented that?

Define Your Non-Negotiables

These are the boundaries you must uphold to maintain your well-being. Some examples include:

- "I won't answer work emails after 7:00 p.m."
- "I don't tolerate gossip or negativity about people I care about."
- "I need at least one night a week to recharge alone."

Protecting Your Boundaries

Once you've defined your boundaries, it's important to communicate and protect them. Here's how:

- **Be clear:** Use simple, direct language to express your boundaries.

- Example: "I need time to recharge after work, so I'll call you back tomorrow."
- **Stay firm:** Don't backtrack or over-explain. Your boundaries are valid, period.
  - Example: "I can't lend you money right now—that's just not an option."
- **Anticipate pushback:** Some people may test your boundaries. Stay calm and consistent.
  - Example: "I understand your frustration, but my decision is final."

Respecting Others' Boundaries

Boundaries are a two-way street. Just as you want your boundaries respected, it's essential to honor others' limits.

- **Listen actively:** When someone expresses a boundary, take it seriously.
- **Avoid guilt-tripping:** Respect their decision without trying to change their mind.
- **Check in:** If you're unsure, ask: "Is this okay with you?"

Boundaries aren't walls—they're bridges to healthier, more balanced relationships. Remember, setting boundaries isn't selfish —it's self-respect in action. And every time you reinforce a boundary, you reinforce the message that you deserve kindness, respect, and care.

INTERACTIVE ELEMENT: LOVE M(E)USINGS

Grab your favorite journal, light a candle, and pour yourself a cup of tea—it's time for some heartfelt reflection. These journal prompts are designed to help you explore your emotions, uncover hidden truths, and learn how to manage them with grace and self-compassion. Write freely and honestly; there's no right or wrong way to do this. Let your pen lead you toward understanding and growth.

1. **What emotion have I been feeling most often lately?**
   - Describe it in detail. Where do you feel it in your body? What triggers it?
2. **What do my emotions teach me about what I need right now?**
   - Is it rest, connection, or something else entirely?
3. **How do I know when I'm approaching my emotional limits?**
   - What signs does my body or mind give me, and how can I respond with self-care?
4. **What are some boundaries I need to set to protect my emotional well-being?**
   - Who or what do I need to say no to more often?
5. **What's one emotion I've been avoiding or suppressing? Why?**
   - What would it feel like to acknowledge and process this emotion?
6. **How do I show kindness and compassion to others?**
   - How can I extend that same kindness to myself?
7. **What past experience has shaped the way I handle my emotions today?**
   - How can I use this awareness to grow?
8. **What does emotional freedom look and feel like to me?**
   - Paint a picture with your words of a life where you handle emotions with confidence and ease.

9. **What's a memory of a time I handled a tough situation with grace?**
   - What skills or strengths did I use, and how can I apply them now?
10. **Who or what makes me feel emotionally supported?**
    - How can I nurture these connections more intentionally?
11. **What are three ways I can ground myself when my emotions feel overwhelming?**
    - List practical techniques, like breathing exercises, journaling, or calling a friend.
12. **What's a non-negotiable boundary I need to enforce more firmly?**
    - How will enforcing it protect my energy and peace?
13. **If I could give my emotions a voice, what would they say to me right now?**
    - Write as if your emotions were speaking directly to you —what do they need you to know?

INTERACTIVE ELEMENT: MAKING YOUR SAFE SPACE

Your environment has a powerful impact on your emotions, energy, and overall well-being. Creating a safe space isn't just about tidying up—it's about designing a haven where you can relax, recharge, and reconnect with yourself. Whether it's an entire room, a cozy corner, or even a portable safe space you carry in your bag, this activity will guide you step-by-step to craft a calming environment that feels uniquely yours.

Step 1: Choose Your Space

Decide where your safe space will be. It doesn't need to be big or fancy—it just needs to feel like yours.

Options:

- A corner of your bedroom or living room
- A specific chair, nook, or even your bed
- A portable bag of items that bring you comfort for when you're on the go

Step 2: Declutter and Simplify

Clutter can make you feel overwhelmed and distracted, so start by clearing unnecessary items from your chosen space.

Tips:

- Remove anything that doesn't serve a purpose or bring you joy.
- Keep only items that feel calming, meaningful, or practical.
- Mindset tip: Letting go of physical clutter can be symbolic of releasing emotional clutter.

Step 3: Add Comfort

Your safe space should feel like a warm hug, so focus on adding elements that bring comfort.

Ideas:

- **Soft textures:** Add a cozy blanket, cushions, or a plush rug.
- **Comfortable seating:** A supportive chair, beanbag, or even a pile of pillows works great.
- **Warm lighting:** Use fairy lights, candles, or a soft lamp to create a calming glow.

Step 4: Engage Your Senses

Incorporate sensory elements to ground yourself and create a calming atmosphere.

Suggestions:

- **Sight:** Choose soothing colors (like blues or greens) and add personal touches, like photos or artwork.
- **Smell:** Use essential oils, scented candles, or fresh flowers for a pleasant aroma.
- **Sound:** Create a playlist of calming music or nature sounds, or keep a white noise machine or portable speaker nearby.
- **Touch:** Include textures that feel good to you, like a soft blanket or a squishy stress ball.
- **Taste:** Keep a stash of your favorite calming teas, mints, or snacks.

Step 5: Personalize It

Make your safe space uniquely yours by adding items that bring joy, inspiration, or peace.

Ideas:

- A journal or sketchbook
- A few favorite books
- Inspirational quotes or affirmations
- A small plant or crystal for a touch of nature
- Mementos that remind you of happy memories

Step 6: Keep It Accessible

Your safe space should be easy to use whenever you need it.

Tips:

- Keep frequently used calming tools (like a journal or meditation app) within arm's reach.
- If your safe space is portable, use a bag or box to store everything neatly.

Step 7: Use Your Safe Space Intentionally

Your safe space is there to support you—but it's up to you to use it.

How to Use It:

- Retreat to your space during moments of stress, overwhelm, or sadness.
- Use it for calming rituals like meditation, journaling, or reading.
- Spend a few minutes each day in your space to recharge, even when you're not feeling overwhelmed.

Helpful Tips for Maintaining Your Safe Space

- **Keep it tidy:** Regularly declutter and clean your space to maintain its calming energy.
- **Refresh it seasonally:** Swap out elements to match the season—like lighter blankets in summer or a new scent in fall.
- **Set boundaries:** Let others in your household know this space is yours and needs to be respected.

Creating a safe space is a powerful way to nurture yourself. It's not about perfection—it's about designing a space that feels calming, supportive, and uniquely you. As you settle into your sanctuary, take a deep breath and remind yourself: This is your place to pause, reflect, and reconnect with the amazing person you are. You deserve this space—and the peace it brings.

You've just taken a huge step toward becoming your own biggest supporter! These tools aren't just concepts; they're the foundation of a life filled with unstoppable confidence, emotional freedom, and lasting self-compassion.

But the journey doesn't stop here. In the next chapter, we'll take everything you've learned and dive even deeper. Together, we'll explore essential DBT exercises that will empower you to manage your emotions more effectively, reduce stress, and strengthen your relationships—both with others and, most importantly, with yourself.

Get ready to take your emotional toolkit to the next level. Your unstoppable self is just getting started!

CHAPTER 5: HANDLE WITH CARE

A DBT TOOLBOX FOR SELF-COMPASSION

 Let go or be dragged.

— ZEN PROVERB

You are not a problem to be solved—you're a work in progress, and even masterpieces need some care. This chapter is here to help you do just that. Think of it as a toolbox for managing emotions, reducing stress, and building stronger relationships—with others and, most importantly, yourself.

Self-compassion isn't just a nice idea; it's the key to emotional freedom and unstoppable confidence. This chapter will guide you through simple, effective DBT techniques to quiet your inner critic, handle tough emotions, and give yourself the kindness you deserve.

Let's unpack these tools together so you can handle life with grace and show yourself the care you've always deserved. Ready?

DISTRESS TOLERANCE: WEATHERING THE STORM

In the previous chapter, we discussed distress tolerance and the set of techniques it uses to help us handle uncomfortable situations and difficult emotions without becoming overwhelmed. Here, I am including one activity and one worksheet for "weathering the storm" using distress tolerance.

Activity: Riding the Wave—Weathering the Storm of Intense Emotions

In this exercise, we will explore ways to recognize and manage intense emotions using the concept of "riding the wave." This will help you handle uncomfortable situations without being overwhelmed, empowering you to build lasting resilience.

Objective: To facilitate your ability to observe and let emotions pass naturally while grounding yourself.

Instructions:

1. **Pause and notice:** When you feel overwhelmed, take a moment to pause. Identify the feeling you are experiencing without judgment.
   - Example: "I feel sadness rising in my chest. It's heavy, but it's okay."
   - Feeling:
2. **Name the emotion:** Say out loud or write down the emotion. Naming it helps to externalize it and reduce its power.
   - Emotion:
3. **Ride the wave:** Visualize your emotion as a wave in the ocean. Acknowledge its rise and fall, understanding that no wave lasts forever. Use this moment to breathe deeply.
   - Count your inhales and exhales:
     - Inhale for a count of four.
     - Hold for four.
     - Exhale for six.
4. **Ground Yourself:** Use the 5-4-3-2-1 technique to reconnect with the present. Fill in the blanks:
   - 5 things I see:
   - 4 things I can touch:
   - 3 things I can hear:
   - 2 things I can smell:
   - 1 thing I can taste:
5. **Reflect:** After the wave subsides, reflect on your experience:
   - The emotion was (circle one): intense / manageable / mild.
   - Did the wave pass? □ Yes □ No
   - How do you feel now compared to before?

By combining these exercises, you're equipped to embrace your emotions, fostering a sense of emotional freedom and self-compassion. Remember, you have the strength to ride the waves of life!

CREATING YOUR INNER SAFE SPACE: A UNIQUE JOURNEY INWARD

Imagine a sanctuary within you—a space where you can retreat anytime life feels overwhelming. This exercise will guide you step-by-step to design your inner safe space, a place of comfort, strength, and calm that exists entirely in your mind. Unlike a physical space, this one is always accessible, no matter where you are or what's happening around you. Let's begin.

Step 1: Envision the Surroundings

Start by imagining what your ideal safe space looks like. There are no rules—it could be a cozy cabin in the woods, a sunlit meadow, or even a room filled with soft pillows and twinkling lights. Close your eyes and take a moment to picture it.

- What colors make you feel calm and happy?
- Are there objects that bring you comfort? Maybe your favorite blanket, a glowing candle, or a childhood keepsake?
- Is it indoors, outdoors, or a mix of both?

Write down what you see in your journal. The more details, the better. This is your personal retreat, and it should reflect what makes *you* feel safe and at ease.

Step 2: Activate Your Senses

Bring your space to life by engaging your senses. Imagine the sounds, scents, textures, and even tastes that make this space feel perfect.

- **Sound:** Is there soft music playing? Do you hear waves crashing, birds chirping, or the crackling of a fireplace?
- **Scent:** What smells calm you? Lavender? Fresh rain? A warm cup of tea? Imagine those scents filling your space.
- **Touch:** Think about how everything feels. Is there a plush rug underfoot, a silky blanket, or the warmth of the sun on your skin?
- **Taste:** Maybe there's a comforting cup of tea, your favorite snack, or fresh fruit nearby.

Imagine yourself fully immersed in this sensory experience.

Step 3: Choose an Anchor Activity

What activity would you do in this space that grounds and soothes you? Choose something that helps you feel connected and calm.

- Journaling your thoughts.
- Drawing or painting something playful and imperfect.
- Practicing slow, deep breaths or gentle yoga stretches.
- Simply sitting in stillness and letting your mind wander.

Pick an activity you can visualize yourself doing in your safe space.

Step 4: Cultivate a Supportive Inner Voice

This safe space is only as peaceful as the thoughts you bring into it. Practice replacing self-criticism with supportive, encouraging inner dialogue. Imagine a kind, compassionate version of yourself speaking to you in this space.

- What words of encouragement or comfort would you want to hear?
- How would your inner voice reassure you in difficult moments?

Write down one or two affirmations that you'll carry into this space, like:

- "I am safe here."
- "It's okay to feel what I'm feeling."
- "I am enough, exactly as I am."

Step 5: Practice Emotional Grounding

Once your space feels complete, practice grounding yourself in it during moments of stress or uncertainty. Here's how:

1. Close your eyes and take a deep breath.
2. Visualize your safe space in vivid detail.
3. Imagine yourself walking into it, feeling the calm wash over you.
4. Engage your senses one by one—what do you see, hear, feel, smell, and taste?
5. Remind yourself: "This space is always within me."

When you're ready, open your eyes, knowing you can return to this space anytime.

After creating and practicing in your inner safe space, take a moment to reflect and write in your journal.

- How did it feel to imagine and ground yourself there? Write down any thoughts or insights you have about the experience.

This inner safe space isn't just an escape—it's a tool for resilience, self-compassion, and emotional freedom. It's a reminder that no matter what's happening outside, there's a calm, supportive place you can always return to within yourself.

DBT WORKSHEET: MANAGING EMOTIONS WITH THE STOP METHOD

This worksheet is designed to help you pause, reflect, and respond to challenging emotions in a healthier way using the STOP Method—a powerful DBT tool for emotional regulation.

STOP stands for:

- **S**top
- **T**ake a step back
- **O**bserve
- **P**roceed mindfully

When emotions feel overwhelming, this method helps you interrupt impulsive reactions and choose a more thoughtful response.

Exercise: Practice the STOP Method

Stop

Take a moment to pause. Resist the urge to act immediately, especially if you're feeling overwhelmed or reactive. Imagine hitting the pause button.

- What triggered your emotion? Write it down.

Take a Step Back

Physically or mentally step back from the situation. This helps create space between you and the intensity of the emotion.

- How did you step back?
  - ☐ Left the room
  - ☐ Took a few deep breaths
  - ☐ Counted to ten
  - ☐ Other

Observe

Take a moment to notice what's happening inside and around you. This includes:

- **Body:**
  - What physical sensations are you feeling?
    - ☐ tense muscles
    - ☐ racing heart
    - ☐ heavy chest
    - ☐ other
- **Mind:**
  - What thoughts are running through your mind?
- **Emotion:**
  - Name the emotion you're experiencing (e.g., anger, sadness, frustration).
- **Environment:**
  - What's happening in your surroundings?

Proceed Mindfully

Once you've paused, stepped back, and observed, choose your next action mindfully. This means acting in a way that aligns with your values and long-term goals rather than reacting impulsively.

- **Ask Yourself:**
  - What outcome do I want from this situation?
  - What action will help me achieve that?

Reflection:

- How did it feel to use the STOP method in this situation?
- What did you learn about your emotions or reactions?

Bonus Tip: Practice Makes Progress

The STOP method takes practice. Consider revisiting this worksheet anytime you face a difficult emotion to strengthen your ability to respond thoughtfully. Over time, you'll notice more control over your emotions and reactions.

DBT EXERCISES FOR INTERPERSONAL EFFECTIVENESS: DEARMAN, GIVE, AND FAST

Below are three DBT exercises, each designed to help you practice and strengthen key skills for improving communication and maintaining healthy relationships.

DEARMAN Exercise: Assert Your Needs

Objective: Practice using the DEARMAN technique to assertively communicate your needs while staying respectful and effective. This acronym stands for (Linehan, 2015):

- **D**escribe the situation: Clearly and objectively describe what's happening.
- **E**xpress your feelings: Share how the situation impacts you.
- **A**ssert your needs: State what you want or need clearly and respectfully.
- **R**einforce: Explain why fulfilling your request benefits the other person.
- **M**indful: Stay focused on your goal despite distractions or pushback.
- **A**ppear confident: Use confident body language and tone.
- **N**egotiate: Be willing to compromise if necessary.

Instructions:

1. Think of a recent situation where you felt your needs weren't being met or your boundaries were crossed.
2. Use the DEARMAN framework to write out how you could have communicated effectively.

Example Template:

- **Describe:** "Yesterday, when you interrupted me during the meeting, I felt like I wasn't able to share my ideas."
- **Express:** "I felt frustrated because I value being heard."
- **Assert:** "I'd appreciate it if you could let me finish my thoughts before responding."

- **Reinforce:** "When we both get a chance to share, it helps us collaborate better."
- **Mindful:** *I'll focus on staying calm and not getting distracted by any negative reactions.*
- **Appear confident:** *I'll maintain steady eye contact and speak in a firm tone.*
- **Negotiate:** "If you feel like I'm talking too long, let's agree on a signal to let me know."

Reflection:

- How did it feel to write out your DEARMAN script?
- What would you change if you were to use this approach in the future?

GIVE Exercise: Build Relationships

Objective: Practice the GIVE skill to nurture and strengthen important relationships. This acronym stands for (*Relationship Effectiveness: GIVE*, n.d.):

- **Gentle:** Use a gentle tone and avoid criticism or harsh words.
- **Interested:** Show genuine interest in the other person's perspective.
- **Validate:** Acknowledge the other person's feelings or experiences.
- **Easy manner:** Keep the conversation light, relaxed, and approachable.

Instructions:

- Identify someone you want to improve your relationship with (e.g., a friend, partner, or coworker).
- Write out a plan to use GIVE in a conversation with them.

Example Template:

- **Gentle:** "I noticed you seemed upset earlier—I hope everything's okay."
- **Interested:** "How are you feeling about what happened? I'd really like to understand."
- **Validate:** "It makes sense that you'd feel hurt. That's a lot to deal with."
- **Easy manner:** *Smile softly, nod, and keep your tone calm and open.*

Reflection:

- Did using GIVE help improve your interaction?
- How did the other person respond to your approach?

FAST Exercise: Maintain Self-Respect

Objective: Use the FAST skill to maintain your self-respect while interacting with others. The acronym stands for (Charlie Health Editorial Team, 2023):

Fair: Be fair to both yourself and the other person.

Apologies: Don't over-apologize or apologize unnecessarily.

Stick to values: Stay true to your values, even if it's uncomfortable.

Truthful: Be honest and avoid exaggerations or excuses.

Instructions:

- Think of a situation where you struggled to maintain self-respect during a difficult conversation.
- Use the FAST framework to rewrite how you could approach it differently.

Example Template:

- **Fair:** "I know you're upset, and I also deserve to have my perspective considered."
- **Apologies:** Instead of over-apologizing,
  - Say: "I understand your frustration and want to find a solution."
  - Avoid: "I'm sorry I exist; I'll never speak again!"
- **Stick to values:** "It's important to me to address this calmly, without blaming each other."
- **Truthful:** "I made a mistake in how I handled this, and I want to make it right."

Reflection:

- How did the FAST approach feel compared to how you normally handle similar situations?
- What did you notice about your self-respect during and after the exercise?

Practicing DEARMAN, GIVE, and FAST helps you balance your needs, relationships, and self-respect. These tools take practice but can transform how you manage conversations and conflicts. Printable copies of these exercises can be downloaded from Self-Love.LeighWHart.com. Keep these worksheets handy and revisit them as needed!

You've done the work, dived into the exercises, and discovered that managing emotions and building stronger relationships starts with treating yourself with care. You've added powerful tools to your self-compassion toolbox—tools that will help you weather life's storms, communicate more effectively, and maintain your self-respect no matter what comes your way.

In the next chapter, we'll explore a whole new way to connect with yourself—through art. No, you don't need to be an artist or even know how to draw a straight line! It is time to discover how creativity can unlock deeper insights, process emotions, and build a bridge between your inner world and your outward expression.

Embracing Your Journey and Inspiring Others

Your task is not to seek for love, but merely to seek and find all the barriers within yourself that you have built against it.

— *RUMI*

You are doing a lot of work here, and it's important to acknowledge the dedication you've shown in cultivating self-compassion through Mindfulness-Based Stress Reduction (MBSR) and Dialectical Behavior Therapy (DBT). Your commitment to these practices reflects a profound investment in your well-being and personal growth.

Self-love is a continuous journey, essential for leading a fulfilling life. By embracing self-compassion, you lay the foundation for resilience and inner peace. Continuing this work enhances your relationship with yourself and enriches your interactions with others.

Celebrating your progress is vital. Recognizing your achievements reinforces positive change and motivates further development. As you embody self-love, you become a beacon for others, demonstrating the power of radical self-compassion. Your journey can inspire those around you to embark on their own paths toward self-acceptance.

If this book has supported you in any way—by offering new insights, providing coping tools, or opening your heart to self-love—please consider sharing your experience. Writing a review not only assists others in discovering this resource but also serves as a testament to your growth, inspiring others to begin their own journeys.

Your feedback is invaluable. Reviews contribute to the visibility and credibility of this work, enabling it to reach and assist a broader audience. Your voice can make a difference in someone else's path toward self-love.

Thank you so much for your support.

Now turn the page to discover healing and creative art therapy and narrative therapy exercises designed to deepen your self-love practice.

Scan the QR code to leave your review on Amazon

MODALITY THREE

ART THERAPY

CHAPTER 6: DRAWING INWARD

ART THERAPY FOR SELF-CONNECTION

 Art washes away from the soul the dust of everyday life.

— *PABLO PICASSO*

When was the last time you picked up a crayon or doodled just for fun? Not to impress anyone, not to create something Instagram-worthy, but just to let your hands wander and see what came out? For most of us, it's been a while—and honestly, that's a shame. Because deep down, we all have a part of ourselves that craves the freedom to color outside the lines, to create without judgment, and to reconnect with that curious, creative side we so often bury under responsibility, fear, or self-doubt.

In this chapter, we're diving into the beautiful, messy, and liberating world of art therapy. I'm here to guide you through how creative self-expression can unlock emotions you didn't even know were tucked away and help you gain clarity about who you are.

Let's draw inward, shall we? Because the masterpiece of your life isn't just about what you create—it's about discovering you in the process.

THE POWER OF ART: A LIFELINE FOR MENTAL HEALTH

Art has this magical ability to bypass all the noise in our heads— the endless to-do lists, the self-criticism, the "what ifs"—and go straight to the heart of what we're feeling. It's like an emotional translator, taking all those buried, unspoken thoughts and turning them into something visible, tangible, and real. And that is where its power lies.

Science backs this up, too. Studies show that creative self-expression can reduce anxiety, improve mood, and even lower levels of stress hormones like cortisol (Godreau, 2024). Engaging in art isn't just a fun distraction; it's an active way to support your mental health. When you allow yourself to create without judgment, you give your brain a chance to relax, your emotions a way to flow, and your inner critic a much-needed time-out.

Self-Expression: Your Secret Weapon

Think about it: How often do we bottle up our feelings, plaster on a smile, and keep going because, well, life demands it? Art offers a space where you don't have to do that anymore. It's a space where you can be raw, messy, and completely yourself.

When you express yourself through art, you're giving your emotions a safe outlet. Sadness, anger, joy, hope—they all belong here. Scribbling in frustration or painting in peace becomes a way of releasing tension, processing pain, and even celebrating the small wins you might overlook otherwise. You don't have to explain yourself or make sense to anyone but you.

Benefits Beyond the Brushstrokes

The beauty of art therapy is that its benefits extend far beyond the canvas (or sketchpad or piece of paper you're working on). Here's what happens when you make space for creative expression in your life:

- **Clarity:** By putting your emotions into shapes, colors, or lines, you start to understand yourself on a deeper level. Sometimes, your art can reveal things you didn't even realize you were feeling.
- **Stress relief:** The simple act of focusing on a creative task has a meditative effect. You might notice your breathing slows, your shoulders relax, and the world feels just a little less overwhelming.
- **Resilience:** Art helps you explore your strengths and your struggles in a safe way. Over time, it can build your emotional resilience, giving you tools to face challenges with more confidence.
- **Connection:** While art therapy is often a deeply personal experience, sharing your creations (if and when you're ready) can foster connection and understanding with others.

Art as Your Personal Compass

Art doesn't just help you cope; it helps you manage. By creating, you're charting a path to greater self-awareness, self-compassion, and emotional freedom. You're giving yourself permission to feel without fear, to grow without pressure, and to heal in a way that feels uniquely yours.

So why not lean into this creative process? You don't need to be an artist to access the power of art therapy. All you need is an open mind, a little courage, and maybe a box of markers you forgot was hiding in the back of your closet. Your mental health—and your heart—will thank you.

COLORS AND EMOTIONS: PAINTING YOUR INNER WORLD

Have you ever noticed how a bright yellow room can feel energizing while a soft blue one feels calming? Or how a fiery red dress can make you feel bold, while wearing gray might make you feel a little... meh? Colors are powerful communicators of emotion, both in the art we create and in the world around us. In art therapy, color becomes a tool—almost like a language—for expressing feelings we might not be able to put into words.

The Psychology of Color

Color psychology explores the connection between colors and how they affect our minds and emotions. It's fascinating how certain hues can evoke specific feelings, both consciously and subconsciously. Here's a quick rundown of what some common colors might convey:

- **Red:** Passion, energy, anger, or excitement. It's a color that grabs attention and doesn't let go.
- **Blue:** Calmness, serenity, or sometimes sadness. It's the color of the sky and sea, often grounding and reflective.
- **Yellow:** Joy, optimism, and warmth. Think sunshine—it's hard not to feel uplifted by a splash of yellow.
- **Green:** Balance, growth, and renewal. It's a color that often connects us to nature and healing.

- **Purple:** Creativity, mystery, and spirituality. Purple can feel both luxurious and introspective.
- **Black:** Power, mystery, or mourning. It's bold yet often a place of safety and reflection.
- **White:** Purity, simplicity, or a clean slate. It can feel refreshing but also isolating at times.

Of course, these associations can vary depending on culture, personal experiences, and even the shades or combinations of colors used.

The Role of Color in Art Therapy

When we create art, the colors we choose aren't random—they're often deeply connected to our emotions. For instance, if you're feeling frustrated, you might unconsciously reach for bold, jagged strokes of red or black. If you're seeking peace, soft blues, and greens might make their way onto your canvas.

In art therapy, paying attention to the colors you naturally gravitate toward can provide insight into your emotional state. And the best part? You can also use colors to shift how you feel.

Just as colors can express emotions, they can also influence how we feel. This is why color therapy—a practice that uses colors to promote well-being—has gained popularity in wellness circles. Here are a few ways to harness color in your creative process:

- **Soothing anxiety:** Feeling overwhelmed? Try working with cool colors like blues and greens, which can have a calming effect on the mind and body.
- **Boosting energy:** Need a pick-me-up? Bright yellows, oranges, or even a splash of red can inject a sense of vitality and enthusiasm.

- **Encouraging reflection:** If you're in a reflective or introspective mood, purples and deep blues can help create a contemplative space.
- **Grounding emotions:** Earthy tones like browns and greens can foster a sense of stability and connection to the present moment.

EXPERIMENTING WITH COLOR IN YOUR ART

When it comes to art therapy, there's no right or wrong way to use color—only what feels right for you. Here's a simple exercise to explore the emotional power of color. Grab some markers, pencil crayons, or paint. Whatever you have on hand is fine.

- **Start with a feeling:** Take a moment to check in with yourself. Think about how you are feeling right now.
- **Pick your palette:** Choose colors that you think represent your current emotion. Don't overthink it—let your instincts guide you.
- **Create without rules:** Use these colors to create something abstract in your art journal or on a piece of paper. Let your emotions guide your hand.
- **Reflect on your choices:** Once you're done, take a step back and notice how the colors and shapes make you feel. Do they reflect your emotions, or did they shift them?

By using color intentionally, you can both express and transform your emotions. Whether it's a fiery explosion of red or a serene wash of blue, each stroke is a step toward understanding yourself and connecting with your inner world.

So grab those crayons, paints, or markers and let your emotions spill out onto the page. Your feelings are valid, your colors are yours, and together, they can create something beautifully, authentically you.

THE ART OF SELF-LOVE: A LOOK INTO ART THERAPY

Art therapy is more than just painting a pretty picture or playing with clay. It's a journey—a way to unlock emotions, process experiences, and reconnect with yourself through creative expression. It's about discovering parts of you that might have been buried under layers of fear, stress, or self-doubt and bringing them to light with love and understanding. Let's dive deeper into what art therapy is, how it works, and why it's such a transformative tool for self-love and healing.

Art therapy is a form of psychotherapy that uses art-making as a medium for exploring emotions, resolving conflicts, and fostering personal growth. It's not about creating masterpieces or having any artistic skill—it's about the process of creating and what it reveals about your inner world.

The practice began in the mid-20th century, blending the fields of art and psychology. Margaret Naumburg, often called the "mother of art therapy," believed that creating art allowed the unconscious mind to express itself, similar to the way dreams function in traditional psychoanalysis (Cherry, 2023). Since then, art therapy has grown into a recognized and respected field used in clinical, educational, and wellness settings worldwide.

How Does Art Therapy Work?

Art therapy works by giving you a creative outlet to explore your thoughts and feelings. Here's how a typical session might unfold:

1. **The setup:** In a safe and supportive environment, you're provided with various art materials—paints, pencils, clay, or even digital tools.
2. **The process:** You're encouraged to create something based on your feelings, a prompt, or simply whatever comes to mind. There's no judgment, no "right" or "wrong" way to do it.
3. **Reflection**: After creating, you reflect on what you've made. This might involve discussing the piece with a therapist, journaling about it, or just observing it with curiosity.
4. **Insight**: Through this process, you can uncover patterns, emotions, or thoughts that might have been hidden. These insights can help you process experiences, challenge negative beliefs, and develop a deeper connection to yourself.

Art therapy is often guided by a trained art therapist, but it's also a practice you can explore on your own to supplement your personal growth and self-care journey.

Art therapy can be a powerful tool for addressing a wide range of challenges and emotions. Here are just a few ways it can help:

- **Processing trauma:** Creating art can help externalize painful experiences and provide a safe way to explore and process them.
- **Managing anxiety and stress:** The act of creating is inherently calming and can serve as a mindfulness practice.
- **Improving emotional awareness:** Art helps you tap into emotions that might be difficult to articulate, giving you a better understanding of yourself.

- **Building resilience:** By expressing and confronting emotions, you can develop a stronger sense of self and the tools to handle life's challenges.
- **Enhancing self-esteem:** Seeing your inner world reflected in your creations can foster self-acceptance and a sense of accomplishment.
- **Strengthening communication:** Art provides a non-verbal way to express thoughts and feelings, which can be especially helpful if words feel insufficient.

Common Misconceptions About Art Therapy

Like any therapeutic modality, art therapy comes with its fair share of myths and misunderstandings. Let's bust a few of the most common ones:

- **"I'm not artistic, so I can't do art therapy."** Wrong! Art therapy isn't about creating something beautiful or technically perfect. It's about the process, not the product. Stick figures, doodles, and messy splashes of color are just as valid as intricate paintings.
- **"Art therapy is only for kids."** While art therapy can be wonderful for children, it's equally effective for adults. In fact, it can be especially powerful for adults who've lost touch with their creative side.
- **"You have to be in therapy to use art for healing."** While working with a trained art therapist can deepen the experience, anyone can benefit from using art as a tool for self-reflection and emotional exploration.
- **"Art therapy is just arts and crafts."** This one stings a little because it oversimplifies something truly profound. Art therapy is a structured, intentional process designed to

explore and heal emotional wounds—not just a fun pastime (though it can be that, too!).

Art therapy is, at its core, about showing up for yourself with curiosity and compassion. Each stroke of the brush, each shape molded from clay, is a step toward understanding and embracing who you are. It's not about fixing anything; it's about honoring everything—your struggles, your strengths, your story.

Types of Creative Therapies

Creative therapies encompass a variety of modalities that use art, movement, music, writing, and more to foster emotional expression and healing. Each taps into a different aspect of creativity, offering unique benefits depending on your preferences and needs. Let's explore these incredible options:

- **Dance therapy:** Also known as dance/movement therapy (DMT), it uses body movement to explore emotions, release stress, and connect with yourself. It's not about mastering choreography—it's about letting your body express what words can't. Whether it's swaying to soothing music or stomping out frustration, dance therapy encourages you to feel your emotions physically and reclaim a sense of joy and freedom in your body.
- **Drama therapy:** This involves using role-playing, storytelling, and theatrical techniques to process emotions and gain insight. You can step into a character's shoes to explore difficult feelings or rewrite your story to imagine a brighter future. It's a safe, creative way to confront challenges and rehearse new ways of coping or communicating.

- **Expressive therapy:** This is an integrative approach that combines multiple creative modalities—like movement, art, music, and writing—into one therapeutic process. This holistic approach allows you to explore your inner world from different angles, often leading to deep insights and emotional breakthroughs.
- **Music therapy:** This uses sound, rhythm, and melody to evoke and process emotions. Whether you're listening to music, playing an instrument, or even composing your own songs, music therapy can reduce stress, enhance mood, and foster emotional connection. Don't worry—you don't need to be a musician to benefit; even humming counts!
- **Writing therapy:** This is all about putting your thoughts and feelings into words. Through journaling, letter writing, or poetry, you can clarify your emotions, process past experiences, and imagine new possibilities. Writing helps you give shape to your inner world, making it easier to understand and embrace.

Techniques in Art Therapy

Art therapy involves a wide range of techniques, allowing you to explore whichever form of creativity feels most natural. Here are some popular methods:

- **Collaging:** This involves cutting and pasting images, words, or textures onto a surface to create a visual story. It's a great way to combine elements that resonate with you and explore themes like identity, goals, or emotions.
- **Coloring:** This isn't just for kids—it's a meditative practice that allows you to focus, relax, and let go of stress. Adult coloring books with intricate patterns are particularly effective for creating a sense of calm and mindfulness.
- **Doodling and scribbling:** Sometimes, the simplest forms of creativity are the most freeing. Doodling and scribbling allow you to express emotions quickly and without judgment. It's perfect for moments when you're feeling stuck or overwhelmed.
- **Drawing:** This helps you express thoughts and feelings through lines, shapes, and images. Whether you're sketching a memory, an abstract emotion, or something purely imaginative, drawing is a versatile way to explore your inner world.
- **Finger painting:** There's something wonderfully childlike and liberating about finger painting. Smearing colors with your hands connects you directly to the medium, helping you release emotions and tap into a sense of playful creativity.
- **Painting:** Whether with brushes, sponges, or even your fingers, painting allows you to explore color and texture in a tactile way. It's a great tool for expressing complex

emotions or simply enjoying the soothing motion of brushstrokes.

- **Photography:** This invites you to capture the world through your unique lens. Whether it's snapping a picture of something beautiful or creating a symbolic image that represents an emotion, photography can help you see yourself and your surroundings in a new light.
- **Sculpting:** This involves shaping materials like clay, wood, or stone to create three-dimensional forms. It's a powerful way to explore themes like growth, strength, or transformation—literally shaping your emotions into something tangible.
- **Working with clay:** Clay is forgiving, flexible, and deeply grounding. Whether you're molding a simple shape or creating something more intricate, working with clay encourages you to engage with your hands and release stress while exploring your creativity.

There's no one-size-fits-all approach to creative therapies. You might find joy in scribbling wildly across a page, peace in shaping clay, or insight through writing a heartfelt poem. The key is to let go of judgment, experiment with different modalities, and discover what resonates with you.

Every creative act, no matter how small or simple, is a step toward deeper self-awareness and healing. So, grab whatever materials speak to you—a crayon, a camera, or even a lump of clay—and see where your creativity takes you. It's not about perfection; it's about connection—both with yourself and the limitless possibilities of your inner world.

EMBRACING IMPERFECTION: THE FREEDOM TO CREATE

The pressure to be perfect can be paralyzing. Whether it's in our careers, relationships, or even something as personal as art, the fear of making a mistake often stops us before we even start. But here's the truth: perfection is an illusion, and it's absolutely not required for self-expression. In fact, the messier, the better—because that's where the magic happens.

Art therapy isn't about creating something that belongs in a museum; it's about creating something that belongs to you. It's not about precision but permission—to be yourself, to explore, and to embrace the beauty in imperfection.

Cultivating a Judgment-Free Zone

One of the hardest things to do is quiet that inner critic—the one who whispers, "This doesn't look good enough," or "You're not doing it right." But guess what? In art therapy, there is no "right." Let's rewrite that narrative together with these practical steps:

1. **Shift your focus:** Instead of aiming for a perfect product, focus on the process. Ask yourself, *How do I feel while I'm creating?* rather than, *How does this look?*
2. **Celebrate "mistakes":** That unexpected blob of paint or wonky line? It's part of the story. Lean into the imperfections and see them as opportunities for creativity, not flaws.
3. **Use playful materials:** Sometimes, it's easier to loosen up with materials that feel less "serious." Think finger paints, crayons, or even junk mail for collages.

4. **Set a timer:** Give yourself 10 minutes to create something without overthinking. This time limit keeps perfectionism at bay and encourages spontaneity.
5. **Adopt a curious mindset:** Approach your art with curiosity instead of judgment. Ask, What can I learn about myself through this piece?

Reframing Self-Expression as Fun

Art should feel like an adventure, not a chore. Remember how freeing it was to draw as a child when you didn't care if the tree you sketched looked like an actual tree? That's the energy we're reclaiming here.

Here are some ways to make your creative time more playful:

- **Experiment freely:** Mix materials, use your non-dominant hand, or create with your eyes closed. The goal is to explore, not perfect.
- **Laugh at the chaos:** Smudge paint on purpose. Scribble wildly. Let yourself have a good laugh at the joyful mess you're making.
- **Give your inner critic a name:** When that critical voice pops up, imagine it as a character—maybe a nosy neighbor or a cranky teacher. Politely thank them for their concern and carry on.

The Imperfection Manifesto

To fully embrace imperfection, let's make it official. Here's your permission slip to let go and create freely. Say it with me:

- *I embrace the mess.* Creativity is messy, and that's where its beauty lies. I will allow my hands, my materials, and my emotions to move without hesitation.
- *I release judgment.* My creations do not need to meet anyone's standards—not even my own.
- *I value the process over the product.* What I create doesn't have to look a certain way; it only has to feel like mine.
- *I see beauty in imperfection.* Every smudge, smear, and stray line is a reflection of my unique story.
- *I create for the joy of it.* Art is my playground, not my performance stage.

When you allow yourself to create imperfectly, you're doing more than making art—you're practicing self-compassion. You're giving yourself room to breathe, to explore, and to *be*. Every imperfect stroke is a step closer to embracing your authentic self, and that, my friend, is a masterpiece worth celebrating.

INTERACTIVE ELEMENT: LOVE M(E)USINGS

Creativity blooms when we take the time to reflect, dream, and let our minds wander. These journal prompts are designed to spark your imagination, inspire self-expression, and connect you with your emotions. You can approach them through writing, drawing, or even combining the two—whatever feels right for you!

Creative Writing Prompts

- **A letter to your inner artist:** Write a letter to the creative part of you. What would you say to encourage them? What do they need to feel safe and inspired?

- **Your favorite color's story:** Pick a color that resonates with you right now. Imagine it as a character—how does it feel, move, or interact with the world?
- **The perfect day in your dream world:** Describe a day where everything feels just right. What colors, sounds, and textures fill your world?
- **If I were a shape...:** What shape best represents how you feel today? Write about its edges, curves, or movement and why it feels like *you*.
- **A time I felt most free:** Reflect on a memory when you felt completely free and yourself. What were you doing, and how can you bring that feeling into your life now?

Drawing Prompts

- **Create your emotional weather report:** What does your inner weather look like today? Is it sunny, stormy, or full of rainbows? Draw it out, using colors and shapes to express how you feel.
- **Draw your happy place:** Think of a place where you feel at peace. Whether it's real or imaginary, create a visual representation of this sanctuary.
- **Your inner garden:** Imagine your heart as a garden. What would it look like? Are there wildflowers, trees, or maybe a secret path? Draw whatever comes to mind.
- **Abstract self-portrait:** Use colors, lines, and shapes to represent how you see yourself today. Don't worry about making it realistic—focus on expressing your current mood and energy.
- **The colors of gratitude:** Choose three things you're grateful for and assign each one a color. Create a simple drawing using those colors to represent the joy they bring into your life.

Pick one prompt that calls to you, or combine writing and drawing for a layered expression of your thoughts. You might write about your dream world and then sketch it out, or draw your emotional weather report and journal about what you see. There's no right or wrong way—just let your creativity flow.

Creativity is a bridge—a way to connect with your emotions, express your truths, and embrace yourself with compassion and curiosity. In this chapter, we've explored the transformative power of art therapy, the beauty of imperfection, and the countless ways creativity can heal and inspire.

In the next chapter, we'll dive into hands-on art therapy exercises designed to guide you deeper into your emotions and inner wisdom. It's time to take everything you've learned here and put it into action—playfully, courageously, and wholeheartedly.

CHAPTER 7: ART FOR THE HEART

CREATIVE EXERCISES TO EXPLORE YOUR INNER WORLD

 Art enables us to find ourselves and lose ourselves at the same time...

— THOMAS MERTON

Art has this sneaky way of slipping past the walls we build around our emotions and helping us express things we didn't even realize we were holding onto. It's like your heart has been keeping secrets, and the only way to crack the code is through creativity. Whether you're feeling stuck, overwhelmed, or even a little too comfortable in your comfort zone, art therapy exercises are here to gently nudge (or maybe shove) you into a new space of self-discovery.

In this chapter, we'll explore fun and simple ways to channel your thoughts and emotions into something tangible—something you can look at, touch, and say, "Wow, I made this." From painting your feelings to creating a vision board for your dreams, these exercises are designed to bring out your inner artist and, most importantly, connect you to the deepest parts of yourself.

Remember, there are no rules. No "right" way to do this. This is *your* space to explore, experiment, and maybe even make a glorious mess. So, grab your art supplies—or whatever you have on hand—and let's get started. Your heart has a story to tell, and I can't wait to see the masterpiece you create.

EXERCISES FOR THE SELF-PROFESSED NON-ARTISTS

When someone says "art therapy," it might sound like you need to whip out an easel and channel your inner Van Gogh. But don't worry, this is not that. You don't need a single ounce of artistic talent to dive into these exercises. In fact, I believe the messier, the better—because that's where the magic happens.

Doodling for Beginners

Doodling is one of the most freeing ways to express yourself because it doesn't come with any rules. If you can hold a pen and make a squiggly line, congratulations—you're officially qualified. Think of it as giving your thoughts and emotions a way to move through your hand onto paper. And no, it doesn't have to "look like anything."

Here's how to get started:

1. **Grab your tools:** All you need is a blank piece of paper (or a napkin—no judgment here) and a pen, pencil, or marker. If you're feeling fancy, toss in some colored pencils or highlighters.
2. **Set the scene:** Find a comfy spot and put on some music if that helps you relax. Or, sit in silence and listen to your

thoughts. Doodling can be meditative, so let the vibe match your mood.

3. **Start with a scribble:** Close your eyes (yes, seriously!) and draw a random scribble on the paper. Open your eyes and take a look. Now, turn that scribble into something. Maybe you outline it, add patterns, or fill it in with colors. Let your hand guide you—there's no wrong way to do it.

4. **Try shapes and patterns:** If the blank page feels overwhelming, start with simple shapes like circles, squares, or zigzags. Repeat them. Make them bigger or smaller. Add layers. Watch how your page comes to life with just a few lines.

5. **Focus on feelings:** Not sure what to doodle? Think about how you're feeling and let that guide your lines. If you're anxious, maybe your doodle looks like tight spirals or jagged edges. If you're calm, you might draw flowing waves or soft clouds.

6. **Let it flow:** The beauty of doodling is that there's no pressure to make it "good." You're not making art for anyone but yourself. Let your thoughts wander, and your pen follow. You might be surprised at what shows up on the page.

7. **Reflect (if you want):** When you're done, take a moment to look at your creation. Answer the following questions.
   ◦ What stands out?
   ◦ How do you feel?

This isn't about analyzing yourself like a science project; it's about noticing. Maybe your doodle reveals something you've been holding onto—or maybe it just gave you a moment of peace. Both are wins.

Doodling isn't just kid stuff—it's a powerful tool for mindfulness and emotional release. When you doodle, you're giving your brain a break from overthinking and letting your subconscious do the talking. It's a way to express what words can't and remind yourself that creativity is always within reach.

Word Doodling: Let Your Words Take Shape

Word doodling is a beautiful blend of art and journaling that invites you to explore your inner world using both words and creative expression. Instead of focusing on drawing pictures, you'll focus on drawing *with* words. Think of it as giving your thoughts, emotions, or even your dreams a visual personality. This exercise is perfect for unlocking new insights and, of course, having a little fun along the way.

How to Word Doodle

1. **Pick a word or phrase:** Start with a word or phrase that feels meaningful to you in this moment. It could be an emotion like *hope,* a quality like *strength,* or even a mantra like *"I am enough."* Don't overthink it—whatever comes to mind is perfect.
2. **Grab your supplies:** You'll need a blank sheet of paper and something to write with. Pens, markers, or even a pencil

will work. If you want to add color, keep some colored pencils or markers handy.

3. **Let the word take shape:** Write your chosen word or phrase in the middle of the page. From there, let your creativity flow:
   - Turn the letters into art—decorate them with patterns, textures, or even tiny doodles.
   - Let the letters stretch, curl, or overlap. Play with bold, soft, or exaggerated lines.
   - Add little elements around the word, like flowers, swirls, or stars, that reflect how the word makes you feel.

4. **Expand the story:** Around your main word, start adding related words, phrases, or even questions. For example:
   - If your word is *"peace,"* you might add phrases like *"calm breaths," "sunset walks,"* or *"what does peace feel like to me?"*
   - Use different fonts or styles for each new word— bubble letters, cursive, block letters—whatever feels fun.

5. **Color and connect:** If you want, add some color to your word doodle. Use colors that represent the emotions tied to your words. Maybe peace is soft blues, or strength is vibrant reds. Draw lines, arrows, or shapes to connect words and ideas together—it's like creating a map of your thoughts.

6. **Reflect on your doodle:** Once you're finished, take a moment to look at what you've created. Ask yourself:
   - How does this word show up in my life?
   - What emotions do the colors and patterns bring up?
   - What new connections or insights did this doodle reveal?

Word doodling taps into both the analytical and creative parts of your brain, helping you express your thoughts in ways that feel light and fun. It's a gentle reminder that words carry power, and how you shape them can change the way you see yourself and your world.

The best part? You don't need to be a poet or an artist to do this. You just need a word, some space, and a willingness to play. So, what's your word today? Go ahead—let it come to life on the page.

THE BENEFITS OF CREATIVE OUTLETS: COLORING BOOKS, CREATIVE WRITING, AND MINDFUL PHOTOGRAPHY

When it comes to exploring your inner world, creative outlets can become powerful tools for self-expression, relaxation, and discovery. They help us connect with emotions, find calm amid chaos, and even see life from new perspectives. Let's dive into three beautiful ways to tap into your creativity: coloring books, creative writing, and mindful photography.

Coloring Books: A Path to Calm and Clarity

Remember the pure joy of coloring as a kid? It's time to bring that back—not because it's childish, but because it's therapeutic. Coloring books offer a simple, structured way to immerse yourself in creativity, especially when life feels overwhelming. Coloring is not only fun, but it relieves stress, calms the brain, and relaxes the entire body. On top of all that, it improves sleep and fatigue while decreasing heart rate, body aches, respiration, and feelings of anxiety and depression (Bobby, 2022).

Benefits:

- **Reduces stress:** Focusing on colors and patterns activates the brain's relaxation response, similar to meditation (Bobby, 2022).
- **Encourages mindfulness:** As you choose colors and fill spaces, your mind stays anchored in the present moment.
- **Boosts confidence:** Completing a page gives a sense of accomplishment, no matter your artistic skill level.

How to start: Grab an adult coloring book (or any design that speaks to you) and some colored pencils or markers. There's no right or wrong—use colors that resonate with your mood. Let the repetitive motion of coloring soothe your mind and body.

Creative Writing: Words as a Window to Your Soul

Creative writing is more than just telling stories—it's about giving your thoughts, feelings, and dreams a voice. Whether it's journaling, poetry, or even short fiction, writing allows you to process emotions, explore new perspectives, and tap into your imagination (Mohsin, 2024).

Benefits:

- **Emotional release:** Writing is a safe space to pour out emotions you might not feel comfortable expressing aloud.
- **Fosters self-discovery:** Crafting characters or reflecting on your experiences can uncover deeper insights about yourself.
- **Enhances problem-solving:** Writing helps you untangle thoughts and see challenges in a new light.

How to Start: Pick a prompt like, "Describe a time when you felt truly at peace," or "Imagine a conversation with your future self." Write freely without worrying about grammar or structure. Let your pen (or keyboard) guide you.

Mindful Photography: Finding Beauty in the Details

Photography isn't just about capturing moments; it's about seeing the world in a more intentional, mindful way. Regardless if you're using a fancy camera or your phone, photography encourages you to pause and notice details you'd otherwise overlook.

Benefits:

- **Enhances presence:** Looking for beauty in small moments keeps you grounded in the now.
- **Fuels gratitude:** Seeing the world through a lens helps you appreciate life's tiny, often-missed wonders.
- **Builds resilience:** Photography trains you to find light and beauty, even in unexpected places.

How to start: Take a mindful walk with your camera. Look for textures, patterns, or colors that catch your eye. Snap photos without judgment—this is about the process, not perfection. Later, reflect on what these images reveal about your mood or perspective.

Each of these activities taps into your brain's natural ability to create, explore, and heal. Whether you're filling a page with color, crafting a story, or capturing a stunning sunset, you're giving your mind a much-needed break from the hustle of daily life. These practices aren't just hobbies—they're acts of self-care and self-expression, designed to help you uncover who you are at your core.

So, which one speaks to you today? Let your creativity lead the way—it's waiting to show you just how incredible you truly are.

ART RX: 50 ART THERAPY PROMPTS FOR EXPRESSION AND TRANSFORMATION

Use these prompts and ideas as a starting point to express, explore, and transform using art therapy. You don't have to finish them in one sitting—just start where you feel called and let your creativity guide you!

1. **Emotions in color:** Use colors to represent your current emotions on a blank page.
2. **Self-portrait:** Create a self-portrait that reflects how you feel today—no need for realism.
3. **Mood mandala:** Draw a mandala and fill it with colors representing your mood.
4. **Doodle journal:** Let your pen wander freely for five minutes without lifting it.
5. **Gratitude collage:** Cut out images and words from magazines to create a collage of what you're grateful for.
6. **Word art:** Write a powerful word (like hope) and decorate it with patterns or images.
7. **Emotion masks:** Design two masks—one for how you present yourself and another for how you truly feel.
8. **Vision board:** Collect pictures and phrases that represent your goals and dreams.
9. **Weather feelings:** Draw the weather that matches your current emotions (stormy, sunny, etc.).
10. **Hand of strength:** Trace your hand and fill it with images or words that represent your strengths.
11. **Favorite memory:** Illustrate or collage a moment you cherish.

12. **Life as a tree:** Draw a tree where the roots represent your past, the trunk is the present, and the branches are your future.

13. **Color explosion:** Scribble with your favorite colors to release stress.

14. **Worry stones:** Paint small stones with calming designs or affirmations.

15. **Letter to myself:** Write and decorate a letter of encouragement to yourself.

16. **Emotion mapping:** Draw your body and color where you feel emotions (e.g., blue for sadness in the chest).

17. **Timeline of joy:** Create a visual timeline of your happiest moments.

18. **Dreamcatcher:** Design a dreamcatcher using symbols of what inspires you.

19. **Inner child:** Draw something you loved creating as a child.

20. **Empowerment poster:** Create a poster with affirmations and symbols that uplift you.

21. **Life map:** Illustrate your journey so far with key milestones.

22. **Stress scribble:** Scribble aggressively for one minute, then transform the lines into shapes or images.

23. **Inner garden:** Draw a garden that reflects your current emotional state.

24. **Favorite song:** Paint or draw what comes to mind while listening to a favorite song.

25. **Life boat:** Create a boat filled with things and people that support you during hard times.

26. **Heart map:** Draw a heart and fill it with symbols of what you love.

27. **Comfort zone:** Draw a circle showing your comfort zone and what lies just outside it.

28. **Healing symbol:** Design a symbol that represents healing to you.
29. **Emotion monsters:** Turn your emotions into cartoon monsters or creatures. These can be silly, funny, medieval, whatever comes to mind.
30. **One line at a time:** Add one line to a page daily for a week —see what emerges.
31. **Daily doodle:** Doodle something that represents your day before bed.
32. **Mind maze:** Draw a maze to symbolize a challenge you're navigating.
33. **Freedom wings:** Create wings using colors or symbols that represent freedom.
34. **Favorite place:** Illustrate a place where you feel most at peace.
35. **Reflection pool:** Draw a pool of water and what you'd like to see reflected in it.
36. **Hands of help:** Trace your hands and fill them with people or things that help you.
37. **Circle of energy:** Draw a circle and fill it with colors or images that represent your current energy.
38. **Emotion waves:** Paint or draw waves to represent how your emotions flow.
39. **Life quilt:** Create a "quilt" by filling squares with symbols of important life moments.
40. **Future self:** Draw or collage a vision of yourself 10 years from now.
41. **Rainbow of resilience:** Use a rainbow to symbolize how you've overcome challenges.
42. **Message in a bottle:** Write or draw what you'd send to your future self in a bottle.
43. **Forgiveness path:** Create a path and illustrate what forgiveness looks like to you.

44. **Dream door:** Draw a door and what lies beyond it in your dream life.
45. **Emotion scales:** Draw scales weighing different emotions you're feeling.
46. **Sunrise of hope:** Illustrate a sunrise using colors and symbols of hope.
47. **Grief garden:** Design a garden with flowers representing what you've lost and what you've gained.
48. **Change collage:** Create a collage representing changes in your life.
49. **Balance tree:** Draw a tree with branches for different aspects of your life—work, family, self-care, etc.
50. **Affirmation art:** Pick an affirmation (e.g., "I am enough") and turn it into a piece of art.

MUSIC THERAPY EXERCISE: EMOTIONAL PLAYLIST EXPLORATION

Music has the incredible ability to tap into emotions, soothe the soul, and even help us process what words cannot express. This exercise combines listening to music with creative reflection, allowing you to explore your emotions and gain insights into your inner world.

1. **Set the scene:** Find a quiet, comfortable space where you won't be interrupted. Grab a journal, pen, and maybe some art supplies like markers or colored pencils if you want to get visual.
2. **Choose your playlist:** Create or find a playlist of songs that resonate with different emotions—happiness, sadness, hope, nostalgia, or even frustration. Aim for at least five songs, each evoking a distinct feeling.

3. **Listen intentionally:** Play the first song and close your eyes. Let the music wash over you. Pay attention to how your body feels, what images come to mind, or any emotions that arise.

4. **Reflect and Express:** After the song ends, take a few minutes to reflect and express yourself:
   - **Journal:** Write down what came up for you—memories, emotions, or even just a single word.
   - **Art:** If words don't feel right, grab your art supplies and draw or doodle what the song made you feel.
   - **Movement:** If you're feeling restless, let your body move to the rhythm of the next song, and then jot down how it felt.

5. **Repeat for each song:** Go through each song on your playlist, giving yourself time to reflect and respond creatively.

6. **End with reflection:** When you've finished your playlist, take a moment to look at your journal entries, art, or reflections as a whole. Ask yourself:
   - What patterns or themes emerged?
   - Were there songs that surprised you with how they made you feel?
   - How did this exercise shift your mood or perspective?

Music therapy works because it activates multiple areas of the brain, helping you process emotions in a nonverbal and deeply personal way. Pairing music with journaling or art allows you to express yourself in layers—through sound, visuals, and words. It's a holistic way to connect with your feelings and even release tension or unresolved emotions.

So, the next time life feels overwhelming, press play and let the music guide you. You might just uncover something beautiful about yourself.

CRAFTING AN ART JOURNAL: A STEP-BY-STEP GUIDE TO YOUR CREATIVE ESCAPE

Starting an art journal is like opening a private, no-rules sanctuary where your thoughts, emotions, and creativity can run wild. It's part diary, part sketchbook, and entirely *yours*. Whether you're a seasoned artist or can barely draw a stick figure, an art journal is about expression, not perfection. Let's walk through how to start your own.

Step 1: Gather Your Supplies

You don't need a fancy setup to get started. Here's what you'll need:

- **Journal:** Choose something sturdy with blank or mixed-media pages. A spiral-bound sketchbook or even a plain notebook works great.
- **Art Supplies:** Start with basics like pencils, markers, pens, and colored pencils. Add watercolors, glue, magazines, or anything else that inspires you as you go.
- **Extras:** Scissors, washi tape, stickers, and stencils can add a fun touch.

Step 2: Create Your Space

Find a cozy, well-lit spot where you can relax and spread out your supplies. This space doesn't have to be perfect; it just needs to feel like *yours*. Consider playing soft music or lighting a candle to set the mood.

Step 3: Set an Intention

Ask yourself: *Why am I starting this journal?*

- Do you want to express emotions you're holding inside?
- Are you looking for a creative outlet to unwind?
- Do you want a space to explore dreams and goals?

Write your intention on the first page. It's your guiding light for this practice. Don't worry—it can evolve as you do.

Step 4: Start Simple

Facing that first blank page can feel intimidating. Here are a few ways to ease into it:

- **Backgrounds first:** Cover the page with paint, scribbles, or a magazine collage to create a base layer.
- **Prompts:** Use a prompt like "What does joy look like to me?" or "Today, I feel…" and start doodling or writing.
- **Colors and shapes:** Use your favorite colors and simple shapes to get the creativity flowing.

Step 5: Mix Media and Techniques

An art journal thrives on variety. Don't limit yourself—experiment with different techniques:

- **Doodling and drawing:** Sketch or doodle what's on your mind.
- **Collage:** Glue in pictures, ticket stubs, or anything meaningful.
- **Writing:** Add words, quotes, or affirmations alongside your visuals.

- **Textures:** Use layers of paint, paper, or fabric to create tactile elements.

Step 6: Make It a Practice

Consistency is key, but this isn't about creating every day. Aim for a frequency that feels sustainable—once a week, a few times a month, or whenever inspiration strikes. The important thing is to return to your journal when you need it.

Step 7: Reflect

At the end of each session, take a moment to sit with your creation. Ask yourself:

- How does this page make me feel?
- What did I discover or release during this process?
- What do I want to explore next time?

Step 8: Embrace Imperfection

This is your space to be messy, raw, and real. Your art journal doesn't have to look like an Instagram masterpiece. Scribbles, smudges, and chaos are all part of the magic.

An art journal isn't just a collection of pages—it's a living, breathing extension of you. It grows with you, adapts to your emotions, and becomes a space where you can explore who you are without judgment. So grab your journal, open that first page, and let your creativity take the lead. Your inner world is waiting to unfold.

SIMPLE WAYS TO BE CREATIVE EVERY DAY

Cultivating creativity doesn't have to mean big, time-consuming projects. It's about blending small, joyful moments of expression into your daily life. Here are some easy, approachable tips to keep your creative spark alive every day:

- **Start a daily doodle:** Keep a small notebook handy and doodle whatever comes to mind for just five minutes a day. No pressure to create a masterpiece—just let your pen flow.
- **Make mundane tasks creative:** Turn everyday chores into opportunities for creativity. Arrange your dinner plate like art, fold laundry into fun shapes, or hum a little tune while you clean.
- **Keep a "creative grab bag":** Fill a jar with prompts like "Draw your favorite memory" or "Write a haiku about your morning." Pull one out when you have a free moment and let your imagination run.
- **Try a new perspective:** Do something ordinary in a new way. Write with your non-dominant hand, sketch from a different angle, or take a walk in a new neighborhood. Novelty sparks creativity!
- **Document the small things:** Carry your phone or a small camera and snap pictures of textures, colors, or patterns that catch your eye. Later, reflect on what drew your attention.
- **Free write for five minutes:** Grab a pen and paper (or your phone) and write whatever's on your mind without stopping. This "brain dump" clears mental clutter and makes room for fresh ideas.

- **Play with colors:** Experiment with colors in small ways—use colorful pens, try a vibrant outfit, or mix up your coffee mug collection. Color lifts your mood and encourages playful thinking.
- **Explore music:** Create a playlist of songs you've never heard before. Let the new rhythms and lyrics inspire your mood and thoughts.
- **Practice "what if" thinking:** When faced with a problem or idea, ask, "What if?" What if this chair could talk? What if today's sky was orange? It's a fun way to spark creative storytelling.
- **Celebrate the little wins:** Acknowledge even the smallest acts of creativity—doodling during a meeting, trying a new recipe, or snapping a photo. Every small moment feeds your creative energy.

Creativity flourishes when you make space for it regularly. These small practices remind you that creativity is less about talent and more about allowing yourself to play, explore, and express. Let each day hold a moment of magic—you're more creative than you think!

Remember, these exercises aren't about creating perfect art—they're about creating *you*. With every stroke, scribble, or snap of a photo, you've tapped into your unique way of processing emotions, celebrating joy, and discovering what makes you *you*.

In the next chapter, we'll take this exploration even deeper. It's time to step into the transformative practice of narrative therapy —a chance to rewrite the stories you've been telling yourself and replace them with ones filled with self-love, resilience, and hope. If creativity is the heart of change, your narrative is the soul. Let's craft a story that truly reflects the amazing person you are becoming.

MODALITY FOUR

NARRATIVE THERAPY

CHAPTER 8: REWRITING YOUR STORY

THE SELF-LOVE NARRATIVE

 There is no greater agony than bearing an untold story inside you.

— *MAYA ANGELOU*

Let's talk about the stories we tell ourselves—you know, the ones like "I'm too much," "I'm not enough," or "Why does this always happen to me?" These narratives shape how we see ourselves and the world, often holding us back in ways we don't even realize.

I am here to tell you that you're the author of your story. And if you're holding the pen, you have the power to rewrite it. This chapter is about recognizing the narratives that no longer serve you and reshaping them with compassion and courage.

Narrative therapy is less about ignoring your past and more about reframing it. It's seeing your experiences through a lens that highlights your strength and resilience. Together, we'll dig into those chapters that sting, find the lessons in the mess, and craft a narrative that empowers you to move forward as the bold, unstoppable woman you are.

So grab your courage and a pen, and let's rewrite the story of *you*.

WHY THE STORY WE TELL OURSELVES MATTERS MOST

Have you ever caught yourself narrating your life in your head? Maybe it sounds like, *"I can't believe I messed that up again,"* or *"I keep making the same mistakes."* These inner narratives, whether we realize it or not, shape how we see ourselves and the world around us. They become how we interpret everything—our relationships, opportunities, and even our potential.

Think of it this way: your inner story isn't just a harmless monologue; it's the script you're living by. If that script is full of self-doubt, shame, or blame, it's no wonder you feel stuck, small, or overwhelmed. But what if you could rewrite it? What if the story you tell yourself painted you as the resilient, capable, and worthy woman you truly are?

Our narratives hold incredible power. They influence how we approach challenges, how we treat ourselves, and even how we allow others to treat us. When we're stuck in negative stories—like "I'm always failing" or *"I'll never be good enough"*—it's like dragging around an invisible anchor. But when we rewrite those stories with compassion and truth, we release that anchor and give ourselves permission to rise.

You see, your brain believes the story you feed it. If you tell yourself you're unworthy, it will look for evidence to prove that's true. But when you start telling a story of strength, growth, and possibility, your brain starts finding proof of that too. This is why reframing your inner narrative is so powerful—it's the key to unlocking confidence, emotional freedom, and lasting self-compassion.

The story you tell yourself is the one that matters most because it determines how you show up in your life.

Confronting Your Biggest Critic

If your inner narrative is the script you live by, then your inner voice is the director whispering directions in your ear. For better or worse, it's there—commenting, critiquing, and shaping how you perceive your life. This voice, also known as self-talk, is the constant chatter in your mind. And let's be real: sometimes it's not exactly kind.

Self-talk is the running dialogue we have with ourselves, and it matters because it sets the tone for how we think, feel, and act. Positive self-talk can uplift and motivate, but negative self-talk? That's the biggest critic in the room, always ready to amplify your doubts and insecurities. *"You'll never get this right." "Why do you even bother?"* Sound familiar?

Your inner critic can feel so familiar, so normal, that it starts to feel like truth. It becomes how you see everything—your successes, your failures, your relationships, and even your worth. But just because it's loud doesn't mean it's accurate. Your inner critic often focuses on fears, old wounds, and worst-case scenarios. It's like a funhouse mirror, distorting reality and making you believe the worst about yourself.

When we let this inner voice go unchecked, it becomes an anchor, holding us back from seeing our potential or even enjoying the present moment. But when we confront it—when we call it out for its exaggerations and replace its harshness with compassion—we begin to take back control.

Shifting your self-talk from criticism to kindness is one of the most transformative things you can do. It's not about silencing the voice completely; it's about recognizing it for what it is: a perspective, not a fact. When you approach your inner critic with curiosity instead of judgment, you begin to rewrite the narrative it's been feeding you. And that's when the magic happens—you start seeing yourself as you truly are: resilient, capable, and enough, just as you are.

WHEN YOUR MIND PLAYS TRICKS ON YOU: COGNITIVE DISTORTIONS

Our minds are incredibly powerful. But sometimes, instead of being our greatest ally, they turn into tricksters, feeding us thoughts that are exaggerated, negative, or just plain wrong. These sneaky thought patterns are called cognitive distortions, and they like to distort reality in ways that can leave us feeling anxious, overwhelmed, and stuck.

The good news? Once you know how to spot these mental tricks, you can stop them in their tracks. Let's dive into some common cognitive distortions—and especially those that tend to fuel anxiety—so you can take back the driver's seat from your overthinking mind.

What Are Cognitive Distortions?

Cognitive distortions are habitual ways of thinking that are biased, irrational, or overly negative. They shape how we interpret events and often lead to heightened anxiety or self-doubt (Casabianca, 2024). Think of them as faulty mental shortcuts your brain takes—quick to assume the worst and slow to see the positives.

Here are some of the most common cognitive distortions, complete with examples and how they might show up in your day-to-day life.

Distortions That Love to Fuel Anxiety

Filtering

This distortion acts like a spotlight, focusing only on the negative while ignoring everything else. Did you give a great presentation at work but trip over one word? Your mind might zero in on that one tiny mistake, completely dismissing how well you did overall.

- **Why it fuels anxiety:** It creates a lopsided view of reality where everything feels worse than it is, leaving you stuck in a cycle of self-criticism.

Jumping to Conclusions

This one has two parts: mind-reading (assuming you know what others think) and fortune-telling (predicting a negative outcome without evidence). For example, you might think, *"They didn't text back—they must be mad at me."* Or, *"I just know this meeting is going to be a disaster."*

- **Why it fuels anxiety:** You're reacting to imagined scenarios, not facts, which keeps your stress levels sky-high.

Catastrophizing

The drama queen of distortions, catastrophizing assumes the worst-case scenario in every situation. Got a weird email from your boss? Your mind might leap to, *"I'm getting fired!"*

- **Why it fuels anxiety:** By imagining disaster at every turn, your brain stays in constant fight-or-flight mode, making it impossible to relax.

Overgeneralization

With this distortion, one bad experience turns into a sweeping judgment. For example, "I failed that test, so I'm terrible at everything."

- **Why it fuels anxiety:** It amplifies mistakes and setbacks, making them feel permanent and inescapable.

Personalization

This is when you blame yourself for things outside your control. For example, if a friend seems upset, you assume it's because of something you did.

- **Why it fuels anxiety:** It puts you at the center of every problem, creating unnecessary guilt and stress.

Shoulds

The tyranny of should. This distortion is all about rigid rules, like "I should always be productive" or "I should never make mistakes."

- **Why it fuels anxiety:** It sets impossible standards, making you feel like a failure anytime you fall short.

Emotional Reasoning

This distortion convinces you that your feelings are facts. If you feel anxious, your mind might say, *"If I feel this way, something must be wrong."*

- **Why it fuels anxiety:** It blurs the line between emotions and reality, keeping you trapped in the intensity of your feelings.

Other Cognitive Distortions to Watch For

- **Polarization:** Seeing things as all-or-nothing. ("I'm either perfect or I've failed.")
- **Discounting the positive:** Dismissing compliments or achievements as luck or unimportant.
- **Control fallacies:** Feeling helpless or overly responsible for everything.
- **Fallacy of fairness:** Expecting life to always be fair and feeling outraged when it's not.
- **Blaming:** Either blaming others for your problems or blaming yourself for theirs.
- **Fallacy of change:** Believing others must change for you to feel happy.
- **Global labeling:** Defining yourself or others by a single trait. ("I'm such a loser.")
- **Always being right:** Insisting you're right, even at the expense of relationships.

Now that you can spot these distortions, start questioning them. Ask yourself:

- *Is this thought based on facts, or just my fears?*
- *What's a kinder, more realistic way to see this situation?*
- *If my best friend had this thought, what would I tell her?*

Cognitive distortions might be loud, but they're not the truth. The more you challenge them, the more you can quiet that anxious voice and step into the confident, self-compassionate woman you're meant to be.

NEGATIVE SELF-TALK TO AVOID

Negative self-talk is sneaky, and it takes on different forms for different people. Maybe you've heard these thoughts in your own mind.

Let's review some examples of general self-criticism:

- "I'm such a failure; I always mess things up."
- "I'll never be good enough for anyone or anything."
- "I'm so ugly; no one will ever find me attractive."

What about examples that center around stress?

- "I can't handle this stress; I'm too weak."
- "No matter how hard I try, I can't seem to manage my emotions."
- "Everyone else seems to handle stress better than me; I must be doing something wrong."

There is specific negative self-talk that centers around body image:

- "I hate my body; I'll never feel confident."
- "I'm too fat/skinny to ever look good."
- "My body is so flawed; I avoid things I want to do because of how I look."

Sometimes, it even disguises itself as humor: "I'd lose my head if it wasn't attached!" While these comments seem lighthearted, over time, they reinforce a negative view of yourself.

These thoughts don't come out of nowhere. They're often rooted in past experiences, unrealistic societal expectations, or messages you absorbed during childhood. Maybe someone criticized you, or perhaps you grew up in an environment where perfection was the standard. Either way, negative self-talk becomes a habit—a familiar but harmful way of thinking.

Over time, this inner dialogue becomes a self-fulfilling prophecy. When you constantly tell yourself, "I'll never be good enough," you start believing it. That belief then influences your actions, leading to missed opportunities and a life that feels smaller than it should be.

The good news? You're not stuck with this voice forever. With practice, you can rewrite the script in your mind and cultivate a kinder, more supportive inner dialogue.

LET'S TALK ABOUT NARRATIVE THERAPY

If negative self-talk has been running the show for too long, it's time to try something new—and that's where **narrative therapy** comes in. This empowering approach doesn't just help you silence your inner critic; it helps you rewrite your entire relationship with your thoughts. It's about recognizing that you're not defined by your struggles or shortcomings. Instead, you're the author of your story, and with the right tools, you can create a narrative that uplifts and supports you.

Narrative therapy is a collaborative and non-judgmental form of therapy that helps you separate yourself from your problems. By viewing your challenges as stories rather than fixed truths, you can reshape how you perceive yourself and your life.

Developed in the 1980s by Michael White and David Epston, narrative therapy emerged as a response to more traditional problem-focused therapies. White and Epston believed that people are not defined by their problems but rather by the stories they tell themselves about their lives (Clarke, 2024).

Benefits

- Reduces self-blame and fosters self-compassion.
- Encourages empowerment by highlighting strengths and unique abilities.
- Provides a new perspective on problems, making them feel more manageable.
- Promotes emotional resilience and a deeper understanding of oneself.

Narrative therapy works by helping you identify the stories you've been living by—especially those shaped by negative self-talk—and encouraging you to rewrite them. Through conversation, reflection, and guided techniques, you begin to see yourself not as the problem but as someone capable of overcoming challenges.

Key Techniques in Narrative Therapy

Externalization: The Person is Not the Problem; the Problem Is the Problem

One of the foundational techniques of narrative therapy is externalization, which involves separating yourself from the problem. Instead of saying, "I'm anxious," you might say, "Anxiety is trying to take over my thoughts."

By externalizing the issue, you can look at it objectively rather than letting it define you. This shift allows you to explore how the problem affects your life and what steps you can take to address it —without blaming yourself.

Deconstruction: Breaking Down the Story

Deconstruction involves taking apart the dominant narratives that feel overwhelming or fixed. For example, if you've been telling yourself, *"I'll never succeed because I always fail,"* a therapist might help you explore where that belief came from and challenge its validity.

This process helps you question assumptions and uncover hidden strengths or alternative interpretations that might have been overshadowed by negativity.

Unique Outcomes: Finding Exceptions to the Story

Narrative therapy encourages you to look for moments that don't fit the negative narrative you've been living by. These are the "unique outcomes"—the times you succeeded, showed strength, or overcame a challenge, even if they seem small.

For instance, if your story has been, *"I'm always awkward in social situations,"* a unique outcome might be remembering a time you had a meaningful conversation at a party. Highlighting these exceptions helps you build a more balanced and empowering story about yourself.

When you apply narrative therapy to negative self-talk, it works like this:

- **Recognize the problem narrative:** Identify the negative stories you've been telling yourself.
- **Externalize the issue:** Shift from *"I'm not good enough"* to *"This self-doubt keeps telling me I'm not good enough."*
- **Deconstruct the story:** Break it down—where did this belief come from? Is it really true?
- **Find unique outcomes:** Look for evidence that challenges the negative narrative.

- **Rewrite the story:** Create a new, more empowering narrative that reflects your strengths, resilience, and potential.

Stepping Into Your New Story

Narrative therapy reminds us that our stories are fluid—they can change as we grow, heal, and gain new insights. By reframing your inner dialogue and embracing the idea that you are not your problems, you can step into a narrative of confidence, emotional freedom, and lasting self-compassion.

You are the author of your life. So, grab your metaphorical pen and start writing a story that celebrates all that you are and all that you're becoming.

CULTIVATING A MORE POSITIVE MINDSET

We've all heard the advice to "stay positive," but sometimes life is messy and tough. The goal isn't to fake a smile and pretend everything's fine (that's toxic positivity); it's to embrace an authentic mindset that allows you to see possibilities, find hope, and honor the full range of your emotions.

What Is Toxic Positivity?

Toxic positivity is the idea that you should "just look on the bright side" no matter what, dismissing real feelings in the process. While positivity has its place, this approach can make you feel unheard, invalidated, and even ashamed for experiencing difficult emotions.

Toxic positivity might look like:

- Brushing off feelings: "Just be grateful—it could be worse."
- Forcing positivity on others: "Don't be sad; everything happens for a reason."
- Ignoring problems: "Let's not focus on the negative."
- Feeling guilty for struggling: "I shouldn't feel this way; other people have it harder."

True positivity doesn't deny reality. It acknowledges all emotions, works through challenges and allows for growth.

Tips to avoid toxic positivity:

- Allow space for all emotions. It's okay to feel upset, disappointed, or frustrated. Remind yourself, "It's okay to feel this way right now."
- Replace "at least" with empathy. Instead of minimizing feelings, offer understanding: "I'm sorry you're feeling this way. I'm here for you."
- Practice gratitude without guilt. Focus on small things that bring comfort without forcing yourself to feel grateful for everything.
- Use balanced affirmations. Acknowledge challenges while emphasizing your strength: "This is hard, but I can handle it."
- Ask for help when you need it. Reaching out to a friend, therapist, or loved one can help you process emotions in a healthy way.

Now, let's take a look at tips for creating authentic positivity:

- Reframe, don't ignore. Look at situations from a different angle instead of pretending they're better than they are. For example, shift from "I'll never get this right" to "This is tough, but I'm learning."
- Focus on what you can control. When things feel overwhelming, ask yourself, "What's one small step I can take right now?"
- Celebrate small wins. Whether it's tackling a tough task, drinking enough water, or just getting out of bed, small victories matter.
- Surround yourself with positivity. Spend time with people, activities, and content that uplift and inspire you, whether it's a friend who makes you laugh or a favorite book.
- Practice self-compassion. Treat yourself with the kindness you'd offer a close friend. Remind yourself it's okay to struggle and that you're doing your best.

Cultivating a positive mindset doesn't mean ignoring the hard stuff—it means facing it with grace, hope, and resilience. By allowing yourself to feel all your emotions, reframing challenges, and practicing kindness toward yourself, you can live with less pessimism and more possibility.

True positivity isn't about perfection—it's about progress, authenticity, and growth. And that's worth celebrating every day.

INTERACTIVE ELEMENT: [JOURNAL PROMPTS] LOVE M(E)USINGS

Let's turn self-reflection into a journey of self-discovery. Grab your journal, a cozy corner, and maybe a warm cup of tea. These prompts are designed to gently uncover limiting beliefs and cognitive distortions while helping you rewrite your inner narrative with compassion and love.

1. What is one thought I often tell myself that might not be entirely true? How has this thought impacted my decisions or feelings? (*Example: "I'll never be good enough."*)
2. Think about a recent mistake or setback. How did I talk to myself about it? If a friend made the same mistake, how would I respond to them?
3. What's a story I've been telling myself about who I am (e.g., "I'm too shy," "I'm not creative")? Where might this belief come from, and is it serving me now?
4. When something goes wrong, do I tend to assume it's my fault, someone else's fault, or just bad luck? How does this tendency shape my reactions?
5. Write down three moments from the past month when I felt proud, confident, or capable. How can I remind myself of these feelings during tough times?
6. What is one area of my life where I feel "stuck"? Could my self-talk be contributing to this feeling? If so, how?
7. Are there phrases I say to myself that sound like jokes but might be unkind (e.g., "I'm so clumsy")? How can I reframe these thoughts in a way that's lighter and more supportive?
8. Recall a time when I succeeded despite doubting myself. What did that experience teach me about my capabilities?
9. How do I typically respond to compliments or positive feedback? What does that say about my self-perception, and how can I learn to accept praise more gracefully?
10. Imagine the wisest, most compassionate version of myself giving advice to the me of today. What would that version say about my current struggles, and how would they encourage me to move forward?

Take your time with these prompts. There's no right or wrong way to answer them—just let your thoughts flow. Through reflection, you'll uncover the patterns that shape your self-talk and open the door to rewriting your story with love and self-compassion.

This chapter was all about realizing that you are not defined by your negative self-talk or cognitive distortions. You have the power to rewrite your story—one that reflects your strength, your worth, and the incredible person you are becoming.

In the next chapter, we'll take this even further with practical narrative therapy exercises. You'll dive into hands-on activities to help you reframe your thoughts, externalize your challenges, and rewrite your inner narrative with compassion and purpose. It's time to turn the page on limiting beliefs and start crafting a story that truly uplifts and empowers you.

CHAPTER 9: CHAPTERS OF CHANGE

EXERCISES TO OWN YOUR STORY

 You can't go back and change the beginning, but you can start where you are and change the ending.

— *C.S. LEWIS*

S ometimes, the stories we tell ourselves are less "epic hero's journey" and more "disaster movie meets never-ending rerun." You know the ones I'm talking about—the narratives where you're always the one who messed up, got left out, or just isn't enough. Trust me, I've been there. We all have. But you are not the unchangeable character in someone else's drama. You are the author, and it's time for a rewrite.

In these pages, I'll guide you through exercises rooted in narrative therapy, designed to help you reframe the challenges you've faced and see them as stepping stones to something greater. Think of this as a creative project for your soul: you're rewriting your life story with the care and clarity it deserves. Each exercise is here to help you unearth truths, rewrite limiting beliefs, and step into a story where you're not just surviving—you're thriving.

Write in your journal or use the customized worksheets you can download from SelfLove.LeighWHart.com.

EXERCISE: TELL YOUR STORY

This exercise is designed to tap into your inner wisdom, allowing you to explore your past and present through narrative therapy, fostering deep reflection and self-discovery.

Step 1: Set the Scene

Find a quiet space where you feel comfortable and safe. Remember, this is your time—no distractions allowed.

Step 2: Reflect on Your Life Journey

Think about the significant moments that have shaped who you are today. Here are some thought-provoking questions to guide your reflection:

- **What are the pivotal moments in my life?** Consider both joyful and challenging experiences that stand out.
- **How have these experiences impacted my beliefs about myself?** Reflect on how your self-perception has evolved over time.
- **What emotions do these memories evoke in me?** Allow yourself to feel and acknowledge the range of emotions that arise.

Step 3: Craft Your Personal Narrative

Now, it's time to weave these reflections into your personal narrative. Use the following prompts to help structure your story:

- **Who am I at my core?** Write about your identity, values, and what makes you unique.
- **What stories define my past?** Choose a few key experiences that have significantly influenced your life journey and describe them in detail.
- **How have I grown through my challenges?** Highlight the resilience and strength you've developed through adversity.
- **What are my dreams and aspirations for the future?** Envision the possibilities and articulate your hopes moving forward.

Step 4: Embrace Your Narrative

As you write, remember to be kind to yourself. This narrative is a reflection of your truth, and it's beautiful in all its forms. Allow yourself to celebrate your journey, recognizing the courage it takes to articulate your story.

EXERCISE: THE TREE OF LIFE

This creative and reflective activity will help you visualize your strengths, experiences, and the roots that ground you, leading to greater self-awareness and empowerment.

Step 1: Gather Your Materials

Grab any materials you wish to use to create your tree of life. You can use colored pencils or markers to make this experience fun and vibrant!

Step 2: Draw Your Tree

Begin by drawing a large tree with a sturdy trunk with branches and roots reaching out wide. This tree will represent you, with each part symbolizing different aspects of your life.

Step 3: Roots–Your Foundation

Let's start with the roots of your tree. These are the essential elements of your background, experiences, values, and support systems that have shaped who you are. Reflect on these questions to inspire your roots:

- What values have been instilled in me by my family or culture?
- Who are the influential figures in my life that have supported me?
- What experiences have grounded me during tough times?

Write or draw these roots beneath your tree, anchoring it firmly in the ground.

Step 4: Trunk–Your Strengths

Moving upward, let's focus on the trunk, which symbolizes your core strengths and qualities. Prompt yourself with these questions:

- What are my greatest strengths? Consider both personality traits and skills.
- How do I show resilience when facing challenges? Reflect on moments you've overcome obstacles.
- What do I value most about myself?

List these strengths along the trunk. This is your support system; the sturdy foundation you draw from as you navigate life.

Step 5: Branches–Your Experiences and Aspirations

Now, let's extend those branches! Each branch represents different experiences and hopes for the future. Use these questions to inspire your branches:

- What significant life experiences have shaped me? This could include education, relationships, travel, and so forth.
- What are my dreams and aspirations? Think about where you want to go and what you want to achieve.
- How do I envision my life thriving in the future?

Draw or write about these experiences on the branches, letting them overflow with possibilities!

Step 6: Leaves–Nourishment and Self-Care

Finally, let's add leaves to your tree, which symbolize the nourishment you need to flourish. Consider these prompts:

- What are my self-care practices that rejuvenate me?
- How can I nurture my mental and emotional well-being?
- What activities bring me joy and fulfillment?

Add these leaves to your tree, serving as gentle reminders of what you need to thrive.

Take a moment to step back and admire your tree of life. Reflect on the beauty of your journey, recognizing the resilience and strength within you. Celebrate the unique individual you are!

WORKSHEET: IDENTIFY YOUR CORE VALUES

Understanding what truly matters to you is a powerful step in becoming your own biggest supporter. Let's dive into some insightful questions that will guide you in uncovering your values!

Step 1: Reflect on Your Past Experiences

Let's start by reflecting on experiences that have shaped your values. Ask yourself:

- What moments in my life have filled me with pride? Reflect on achievements, relationships, or experiences that made you feel proud.
- When have I felt most fulfilled and content? Consider the activities, roles, or environments that brought you joy and satisfaction.
- What challenges have taught me valuable lessons? Think about hardships that revealed what truly matters to you.

Step 2: Consider Your Role Models

Next, let's explore the qualities you admire in others. Ask yourself:

- Who do I look up to, and why? Identify people you admire in your life or public figures—what specific traits do they possess?
- What values do they embody that resonate with me? Consider how these admired qualities align with your own beliefs.

Step 3: Visualize Your Ideal Life

Imagine your best life and what it looks like. Pose these questions to yourself:

- What does my ideal day look like? Envision how you spend your time, who you're with, and what values are being honored.
- What legacy do I want to leave behind? Think about how you want to be remembered and what impact you want to have on others.

Step 4: Identify Your Core Values

Now, let's distill your reflections into a clear list of core values. Reflect on:

- Based on my experiences and insights, what values stand out as most important to me? Write down a list of five values that resonate deeply.
- How do these values manifest in my everyday life? Consider specific examples of how you incorporate these values into your decisions and actions.

Step 5: Prioritize Your Values

To clarify what matters most, prioritize your values:

- Which values do I consider non-negotiable? Circle or highlight the top three values above that are essential to your identity.
- How do these core values influence my choices and interactions? Reflect on how embracing these values can empower your journey.

Step 6: Put Your Values Into Action

Finally, think about how you can honor these values moving forward:

- What steps can I take to align my life more closely with my values? Consider small, actionable changes you can implement.
- How can I remind myself of these values daily? Explore ways to incorporate affirmations, visual reminders, or rituals into your routine.

Embrace your core values as guiding lights, and remember, you are absolutely capable of shaping a life that reflects the incredible person you are.

WORKSHEET: TEST YOUR THOUGHTS

This worksheet is all about testing your thoughts, empowering you to challenge negativity and embrace a more positive perspective. Let's get started!

Step 1: Identify Your Thoughts

Begin by tuning into your thoughts. Think about a recent situation or challenge where you felt doubt, fear, or negativity. Ask yourself:

- What specific thoughts are running through my mind in this situation? Write down any negative or critical thoughts that come to you.
- How do these thoughts make me feel? Reflect on the emotions associated with these thoughts—are you feeling anxious, sad, or frustrated?

Step 2: Challenge the Negative Thoughts

Now, it's time to test those thoughts! Use the following prompts to gain clarity:

- What evidence do I have that supports this thought? Consider whether there's any truth to it or if it's mostly fear-based.
- What evidence do I have that contradicts this thought? Reflect on positive experiences or affirmations that challenge the negative belief.
- How would I react if a friend expressed this thought? Picture what you would say to someone you care about facing similar negativity.

Step 3: Reframe Your Thoughts

Let's work on changing those negative thoughts into more empowering ones. Ask yourself:

- What's a more balanced or positive way to think about this situation? Rewrite the negative thought into a more supportive statement.
- How can I phrase this thought in a way that reflects self-compassion? Create a statement that encourages kindness towards yourself.

Step 4: Create Actionable Steps

With your new positive thought in mind, let's explore how to move forward:

- What action can I take to embody this new positive thought? Consider specific steps you can take to support your new mindset.
- How can I remind myself of this positive thought in the future? Think of ways to reinforce this positive mindset, like affirmations or visual reminders.

Step 5: Reflect on Your Progress

Take a moment to reflect on the journey you've just gone through:

- How do I feel after challenging and reframing my thoughts? Acknowledge any shifts in your emotions or perspective.
- What have I learned about my thought patterns? Consider what insights you've gained about yourself.

Remember, you are worthy of love and support—especially from yourself. Keep shining, keep questioning, and keep believing in your incredible journey!

WORKSHEET: EXTERNALIZE THE PROBLEM

This worksheet is designed to help you externalize problems that may be weighing you down. By separating yourself from these challenges, you can empower yourself to find solutions and reclaim your confidence.

Step 1: Identify the Challenge

Think about a specific challenge or problem that's been on your mind. It could be a recurring issue, a fear, or something you feel stuck in. Ask yourself:

- What is this problem I want to address? Write down the challenge clearly and concisely.
- How does this problem make me feel? Reflect on the emotions it stirs within you and jot them down.

Step 2: Externalize the Problem

Now, let's create some distance between you and the problem. Use the following prompts to help externalize it:

- If I were to describe this problem as a character, what would it look like? Imagine how this issue might appear if it were a person or an object—give it a name or a form.
- What qualities does this problem have? Think about its traits—does it feel overwhelming, sneaky, or persistent? Write these down.

Step 3: Understand Its Influence

It's time to explore how this problem influences your life:

- In what ways does this problem impact my daily life? Consider how it affects your thoughts, emotions, behaviors, and relationships.
- What strategies has this problem previously used to hold me back? Reflect on the ways it has tried to keep you stuck or stopped you from pursuing your dreams.

Step 4: Confront the Problem

Now, let's take a stand and confront this externalized problem:

- How would I respond to this problem as if it were a separate entity? Write down how you would talk to it— what advice would you give it?
- What actions can I take to diminish its power over me? List specific steps you can take to create distance or address the issue directly.

Step 5: Transform Your Perspective

Let's reframe your mindset about the problem:

- What strengths do I possess that can help me overcome this challenge? List the qualities or skills you have that contribute to your resilience.
- How can I view this problem as an opportunity for growth? Reflect on the lessons you can learn and the potential for personal growth through this experience.

Remember, the problems you face are not you; they are challenges you can navigate. Keep shining your light and embracing your journey—you're doing wonderfully!

WORKSHEET: EXPLORE YOUR STRENGTHS

Understanding and accepting your unique qualities will not only boost your confidence but also empower you to become your own biggest supporter. Let's dive in and celebrate the wonderful strengths that make you, YOU!

Step 1: Reflect on Your Strengths

Begin by taking a moment to reflect on what you consider your strengths. Ask yourself:

- What qualities do I admire in myself? Think about traits that make you proud, such as kindness, creativity, resilience, or humor.
- What skills do I excel at? List any specific abilities or talents you possess, whether they're related to your career, hobbies, or personal life.

Step 2: Gather Feedback From Others

Sometimes, others see strengths in us that we may overlook. Consider reaching out to trusted friends or family members. Ask:

- What do you think are my greatest strengths? Take note of their responses and any patterns you observe.
- Can you share a memory or story that highlights one of my strengths? This can give you valuable insights into how your strengths are perceived by those close to you.

Step 3: Identify Strengths Through Challenges

Think about the challenges you've faced in life. Reflect on:

- What strengths did I tap into when overcoming obstacles? Consider how you navigated tough situations—what qualities helped you through?
- How have these challenges contributed to my growth? Acknowledge how overcoming difficulties has made you stronger and more resilient.

Step 4: Create a Strengths List

Now, let's put it all together! Create a list of your strengths by answering these prompts:

- List 10 strengths that define who I am. Include qualities, skills, and experiences that resonate with you.
- Next to each strength, write a specific example of how I've used it in my life. This will help you recognize the impact of your strengths in real situations.

Step 5: Visualize Your Strengths in Action

Imagine how your strengths can be utilized moving forward. Ask yourself:

- How can I apply my strengths in various areas of my life? Consider your personal relationships, career aspirations, and self-care practices.
- What new opportunities can arise from embracing these strengths? Dream big! Visualize how your unique qualities can lead to growth and fulfillment.

Keep thriving, keep believing in yourself, and continue being the extraordinary person you are! You've got this!

EXERCISE: WRITE YOUR OWN EULOGY

While this may sound a bit somber, it's actually a powerful opportunity to celebrate your life, values, and the impact you wish to have on others. This exercise serves as a reminder of what truly matters to you and helps you embrace the life you want to live.

Step 1: Reflect on Your Legacy

Begin by considering the legacy you want to leave behind. Ask yourself:

- What values have been most important in my life? Think about what principles you hold dear and want to be remembered for.
- How do I want others to remember me? Consider the qualities, actions, and contributions that you hope will define your memory.

Step 2: Imagine Your Eulogy

Now, let's create your eulogy. Think of it as a celebration of your life. Use the following prompts to guide your writing:

- **Start with a warm introduction.** Imagine a close friend or loved one sharing your name and what made you unique.
    - Example: "Today, we gather to celebrate the life of [Your Name], a vibrant and compassionate soul who inspired everyone she met."
- **Highlight your values and passions.** Write about what you loved and the causes that fueled your spirit.
    - Example: "She dedicated her life to empowering women, advocating for kindness, and spreading laughter everywhere she went."
- **Share stories and memories.** Reflect on specific moments that showcase your strengths or impact on others.
    - Example: "In every challenge she faced, [Your Name] showed incredible resilience, turning obstacles into opportunities for growth."

- **Express the lessons you shared.** Consider the wisdom you wish to impart to those you leave behind.
  - Example: "She taught us the importance of self-compassion, reminding us that we are worthy of love and kindness, especially from ourselves."
- **Conclude with a heartfelt goodbye.** Wrap up with a message that reflects your spirit and encourages others to continue your legacy.
  - Example: "Though she may be gone, her light continues to shine in all of us. Let us honor her memory by embracing life with the same passion and love she did."

Step 3: Reflect on Your Eulogy

Once you've completed your eulogy, take a moment to sit quietly and reflect:

- How do I feel after writing this eulogy? Acknowledge any emotions that arise—whether it be sadness, joy, or inspiration.
- What insights have I gained about my life and legacy? Consider the values and lessons you might want to actively incorporate into your daily life.

Step 4: Live Your Legacy

Now that you've envisioned your legacy, think about how to embody it:

- What steps can I take to live in alignment with this eulogy? Identify specific actions you can incorporate into your life that reflect your values.
- How can I remind myself of this legacy regularly? Consider ways to keep your eulogy's message alive

through journaling, visualization, or sharing with loved ones.

You have the power to shape your story and make a lasting impact. Your legacy is already in motion!

EXERCISE: WRITE A LETTER TO YOU

This uplifting exercise will have you write letters to both your past self and your future self. This powerful practice allows you to reflect on your journey, acknowledge your growth, and set affirmations for the amazing future ahead of you.

Part 1: Letter to Your Past Self

Step 1: Begin Your Letter

Start your letter with a warm greeting. Address it to your past self. Use the following prompts to guide your writing:

- **What would I want to tell my past self about the challenges I faced?** Acknowledge any specific moments that were difficult and express understanding.
  - Example: "Dear [Your Past Name], I know you've faced so many challenges, and it's okay to feel overwhelmed. You are doing your best."
- **What wisdom have I gained that could comfort my past self?** Share insights and lessons that you wish you'd known back then.
  - Example: "Believe me when I say that it's okay to take breaks and ask for help; it's a sign of strength, not weakness."

- **What strengths did I develop through those experiences?** Highlight the resilience and growth you've cultivated.
  - Example: "You've grown so much stronger through these experiences, and each challenge has shaped the incredible person you are today."
- **What encouragement would I give my past self?** Remind your past self of their worth and potential.
  - Example: "Always remember that you are deserving of love and happiness. Keep believing in yourself because brighter days are ahead!"

Step 2: Conclude Your Letter Wrap up your letter with a heartfelt conclusion.

- Example: "With all my love, I'm cheering you on from the future. Keep going; you've got this!"

Part 2: Letter to Your Future Self

Step 1: Find Your Inspiration

Shift your focus to envisioning your future self. Picture yourself thriving and living your dreams!

Step 2: Begin Your Letter

Start this letter with an enthusiastic greeting. Address it to your future self using these prompts:

- **What dreams and goals do I hope to achieve?** Articulate your aspirations for personal growth, relationships, and career.

- Example: "Dear Future Me, I am so excited for all the amazing things you are creating and living out! I hope you've pursued your passion with courage and love."
- **What qualities do I want to remember to embrace?** Encourage your future self to embody certain traits, such as confidence, kindness, or adventure.
  - Example: "I hope you've continued to embrace your strength and compassion. Don't forget to celebrate your accomplishments, big and small!"
- **What challenges do I want to remind you to face with courage?** Acknowledge potential obstacles while reinforcing resilience.
  - Example: "Life may still throw challenges your way, but I know you will face them with the same resilience you had in the past."
- **What affirmations do I want you to hear?** Fill this letter with empowering affirmations to uplift your future self.
  - Example: "You are capable of achieving anything you set your mind to. Trust yourself, and remember to savor every moment of this beautiful journey."

Step 3: Conclude Your Letter End Your Letter With a Heartfelt Message.

- Example: "I'm so proud of you! Keep shining bright and embracing every adventure that comes your way."

Final Reflection

After writing both letters, take a moment to reflect:

- How do I feel after writing to my past and future self? Acknowledge the emotions that arise—allow yourself to feel the love, understanding, and excitement.
- What insights have I gained about my journey? Consider how this exercise helps reinforce self-compassion and awareness.

As we move into the final chapter, let's take all this momentum and turn it into a daily commitment—to love yourself, fully and unapologetically, every single day. Choosing to love yourself is not a one-time decision; it's a practice, a declaration, and an act of rebellion against the doubt and fear that tries to hold you back.

You're ready to close the book on self-doubt and start the next chapter of your life with unstoppable confidence, emotional freedom, and lasting self-compassion. Let's make this the story you've always deserved to live. Onward, with love and power!

CHAPTER 10: THE LOVE HABIT

CHOOSING TO LOVE YOURSELF EVERY DAY

 Love is a choice you make every day.

— *GARY CHAPMAN*

Loving yourself isn't always as easy as it sounds. Life loves to throw curveballs, and some days, just getting out of bed feels like a Herculean task. But self-love isn't about being perfect, and it's not some grand finish line you cross once and for all. It's a daily choice, a practice, a habit—like brushing your teeth or scrolling through your favorite memes before bed.

I'm here to remind you that *you* are worth the effort. Yes, even when you spill coffee on your white shirt, forget your best friend's birthday, or lose your temper during a stressful morning. Loving yourself doesn't mean you'll never make mistakes; it means you'll hold space for yourself when you do.

In this chapter, we're diving into the art of choosing self-love every single day, no matter what. We'll talk about simple ways to build this love habit—practical, doable things you can blend into your life even when you're juggling a million responsibilities. I'll show you how to welcome the messy, imperfect beauty of your journey and stay committed to showing up for yourself, even when life gets chaotic.

Remember, self-love isn't selfish; it's survival. It's the foundation for unstoppable confidence, emotional freedom, and the kind of lasting self-compassion that lights up your life.

HOW TO START A SELF-LOVE ROUTINE

Starting a self-love routine isn't about overhauling your life overnight. It's about creating small, sustainable habits that remind you every day: *I am worthy of care and kindness, especially from myself.* You don't need a guru or a 40-step plan to get started. What you need is a little intention, a dash of consistency, and a whole lot of self-grace.

Here's how you can begin:

- **Start small and simple:** Think of self-love as a muscle. If you haven't been exercising it regularly, you don't jump into a marathon on day one—you take baby steps. Start with one small act of self-love each day. Maybe it's a moment of gratitude in the morning or setting aside five minutes to sip your coffee without distractions. Pick something achievable and build from there.
- **Make it personal:** Your self-love routine should feel like *you*. Forget what Instagram tells you self-care "should" look like. Hate bubble baths? Skip them. Love blasting Beyoncé and dancing in your pajamas? Do *that*. The more your routine reflects who you are, the easier it will be to stick to it.

- **Anchor it to your day:** Find a natural spot in your schedule where you can fit your self-love habit. Maybe it's during your morning coffee, on your lunch break, or right before bed. By tying your habit to something you already do, it becomes easier to remember and harder to skip.
- **Create a ritual:** Turn your self-love practice into a ritual that feels sacred. Light a candle, play your favorite music, or sit in your favorite chair. It doesn't have to be fancy, but adding an intentional touch makes it feel special—like a little love note to yourself.
- **Use visual reminders:** Life gets busy, and self-love can slip off the to-do list. Try leaving little reminders for yourself —notes on the mirror, alarms on your phone, or a sticky note on your laptop that says, "Take a deep breath. You're amazing." These gentle nudges help keep self-love at the top of your mind.
- **Celebrate small wins:** Did you keep your promise to yourself today, even in a small way? Celebrate it! Self-love is about progress, not perfection. Acknowledge your efforts and remind yourself that every step forward is worth celebrating.
- **Forgive yourself when you slip:** You're human. Some days, life will derail your best intentions, and that's okay. Self-love isn't about doing it perfectly; it's about returning to yourself when you stumble. Missed a day? Start fresh tomorrow. What matters is your commitment to showing up again and again.

Building a self-love routine is like planting a garden. It takes time, patience, and a bit of faith in the process. But as you nurture it— watering it with kindness, pruning the weeds of self-doubt—you'll watch something beautiful grow. Start small, stay consistent, and remember: You're worth every ounce of effort. Let this routine be a daily reminder that loving yourself is the best investment you'll ever make.

LIFE-CHANGING SELF-LOVE HABITS TO ADOPT

Building a life rooted in self-love means showing up for yourself every day with habits that nourish your mind, body, and soul. Here are some simple yet powerful self-love practices you can blend into your routine to change how you see yourself and the world around you:

Stop the comparison game: It's tempting to measure your worth against someone else's highlight reel. But let's face it: Comparisons only drain your joy. There's no one else on this planet like you, and that's your superpower. Instead of looking outward, focus inward. Celebrate your growth, your quirks, and your unique path. Redirect that comparison energy toward freedom, and watch your confidence soar.

You deserve kindness: You're doing the best you can, and that's enough. Speak to yourself the way you would a dear friend—with kindness, encouragement, and love. Celebrate your wins, big or small, and remind yourself that you're worthy of love, just as you are.

Others' opinions don't matter: Newsflash: You'll never please everyone, and that's okay! Society's expectations are exhausting, and bending to them won't make you any happier. You have your own values, dreams, and journey—stick to those. What other people think of you is their business, not yours. Letting go of this weight is one of the greatest gifts you can give yourself.

You are permitted to make mistakes: Mistakes aren't failures— they're stepping stones. You don't have to be perfect. Lean into your humanity and let yourself mess up, learn, and grow. Every misstep is a lesson, and every lesson shapes the incredible person you're becoming.

Find the beauty in the simple things: Pause and notice the beauty around you—a blooming flower, the sound of laughter, or the warmth of the sun on your face. Practicing gratitude for life's small joys can shift your perspective and bring more happiness into your daily life.

Your value doesn't lie in your appearance: Your worth isn't tied to a number on a scale, the size of your jeans, or what anyone else thinks about your body. You are valuable because *you exist.* Wear what makes you feel good, move your body in ways that bring joy, and remember that your true beauty comes from within.

Let go of toxic people: Not everyone deserves a front-row seat in your life. If someone drains your energy, disrespects your boundaries, or refuses to take responsibility for their actions, it's okay to step away. Protect your peace—it's a form of self-love.

Feel pain and joy completely: Give yourself permission to experience life's full spectrum of emotions. When you lean into your feelings—whether it's the sting of pain or the warmth of joy—you allow yourself to heal, grow, and savor the richness of being alive.

Process your fears: Fear is a natural part of being human, but it doesn't have to control you. Take time to sit with your fears, name them, and ask yourself what they're trying to teach you. Facing your fears head-on will help you grow stronger and less anxious in the long run.

You are capable of making good decisions: You know yourself better than anyone else. Trust your intuition—it's your inner compass. Even if you make a choice that doesn't work out perfectly, it doesn't mean it was the wrong one. Give yourself the grace to figure things out along the way.

Take every opportunity or create your own: Waiting for the "perfect moment" is a surefire way to keep yourself stuck. Life is happening now. Say yes to opportunities that excite you—or better yet, create your own. Be bold, take risks, and trust that you're capable of amazing things.

You are number one: Prioritize your needs—mental, emotional, and physical. Taking care of yourself isn't selfish; it's essential. Schedule time for rest, hobbies, and moments of joy.

Exercise boldness in public: Speak up. Take space. Assert your voice and presence in the world. Boldness is like a muscle—the more you use it, the stronger it becomes. You deserve to be heard and seen, just as you are.

These habits aren't about being perfect—they're about being intentional. Start small, stay consistent, and trust the process. Every step you take toward self-love is a step toward a more confident, emotionally free, and compassionate you.

JUST KEEP MOVING FORWARD

Personal growth isn't a straight path—it's a winding, bumpy road with unexpected detours and the occasional pothole. Some days, you'll feel unstoppable, like you're making giant leaps. On other days, progress will feel slow, and self-doubt might creep in. That's all part of the journey. The key to staying on the path is learning how to keep moving forward, even when it feels hard.

Here are some tips to help you stay committed to your personal growth:

Embrace Progress Over Perfection

Let go of the idea that you have to "get it right" all the time. Personal growth isn't about being flawless—it's about becoming better than you were yesterday. Celebrate small victories, and remind yourself that every step, no matter how small, is still progress.

Set Clear, Flexible Goals

Goals give you direction, but flexibility gives you freedom. Define what personal growth looks like for you, whether it's improving your confidence, developing new skills, or practicing self-compassion. But don't be afraid to adjust your goals as your needs and priorities change. Life is fluid, and your growth should be too.

Practice Daily Self-Reflection

Take a few minutes each day to reflect on your thoughts, actions, and emotions. Ask yourself:

- *What went well today?*
- *What could I do differently tomorrow?*
- *How did I take care of myself today?*

Reflection helps you stay aligned with your growth goals and recognize your progress.

Prioritize Consistency Over Intensity

It's tempting to dive into personal growth with full force, but lasting change comes from consistent effort over time. Think of it like planting a garden—daily watering and care will yield better results than occasional downpours. Build small, sustainable habits that fit into your life.

Surround Yourself With Growth-Minded People

You are the company you keep. Seek out friends, mentors, or communities that inspire and encourage you. Surrounding your-self with positive, growth-oriented individuals creates a support system to help you stay motivated.

Be Kind to Yourself When You Stumble

Setbacks are inevitable. When they happen, resist the urge to beat yourself up. Instead, view them as opportunities to learn. Ask yourself, *What can I take away from this experience? How can I use it to move forward?* Self-compassion is your most powerful tool in staying on track.

Keep Learning

Growth thrives on curiosity. Read books, take courses, or explore new hobbies that challenge you. Expanding your knowledge and skills keeps your journey fresh and exciting.

Celebrate Milestones—Big and Small

Take time to acknowledge your wins, no matter how small they seem. Did you stick to your self-care routine this week? Did you step out of your comfort zone? These moments deserve celebration—they're proof of your progress.

Stay Focused on Your "Why"

Why did you start this journey? What are you hoping to achieve or become? Keeping your "why" in mind can reignite your motivation when you feel stuck or discouraged. Write it down, put it somewhere visible, and revisit it often.

Remember That Growth Is a Lifelong Journey

Personal development isn't a race; it's a lifetime commitment to yourself. There's no finish line, so take the pressure off and enjoy the process. Some seasons of life will feel full of progress, while others may feel like you're standing still. Both are valid.

The most important thing is to keep showing up for yourself. Even if your steps are small, even if the road feels rough—just keep moving forward. Growth happens not in giant leaps but in the steady accumulation of small, intentional actions. You've got this. One step at a time.

No One Walks This Path Alone

Not one of us walks this path alone – and you have a unique opportunity to help someone else realize that.

Simply by sharing your honest opinion of this book and a little about how it has helped you, you'll show new readers where they can find the guidance to begin their own self-love journey.

Want To Help Others?

Your review can be a beacon of hope for someone who, like you, is seeking a path to lasting self-compassion and unapologetic confidence.

Thank you so much for your support. Sometimes, we all need a guiding light, and your words will make a huge difference.

Scan the QR code to leave your review on Amazon

CONCLUSION

You hold the power to become your own biggest supporter, and that power has been within you all along. Throughout this book, we've walked through what it means to truly love yourself—unconditionally and unapologetically. We've explored why self-love isn't just important; it's essential. When you embrace yourself fully, you open the door to unstoppable confidence, emotional freedom, and the kind of lasting self-compassion that can weather any storm.

Together, we unpacked stress—what it is, how it impacts your mind and body, and how to manage it with mindfulness. You learned how to pause, breathe, and create space for calm, even in life's most chaotic moments. We talked about building your emotional first aid kit—your personal collection of tools, strategies, and reminders to turn to when you feel overwhelmed. And we dove deep into DBT techniques, discovering skills like distress tolerance, emotional regulation, and radical acceptance to help you move through challenges with grace and strength.

Self-compassion became a cornerstone of your journey. You've been learning to silence the inner critic and replace it with a kinder, more understanding voice. You've practiced seeing yourself as you'd see those you love—worthy of support, patience, and love, especially during tough times. This journey isn't about fixing yourself; it's about accepting yourself and working with the incredible person you already are.

Along the way, the exercises and worksheets in this book were here to guide you. They helped you put concepts into practice, reflect on your progress, and build a foundation of growth. These tools aren't just for today—they're yours to revisit anytime you need them. When stress creeps in, when life gets messy, or when you need a reminder of your strength, these pages are here for you.

Take a moment to reflect on how far you've come. Maybe you've learned to pause and breathe instead of reacting. Perhaps you've started noticing the moments when self-compassion replaces self-criticism. Or maybe you've uncovered a strength or resilience you didn't know you had. These aren't just small wins—they're powerful shifts in the way you show up for yourself and the life you're creating.

Whenever you feel like you're slipping or need a reminder, return to this book. Revisit the exercises, pick up the worksheets, and rediscover the power of your own self-love journey. Every step you take toward loving yourself more fully strengthens your foundation and opens the door to greater possibilities.

So, what's next? Are you ready to rewrite your story again? To keep building that life filled with confidence, emotional freedom, and compassion? The journey starts every single day you choose to put yourself first.

You have everything you need within you to create the life you deserve. You've already taken the first steps, and I know you have what it takes to keep going.

Keep showing up for yourself!

Books You'll Love By
Leigh W. Hart

Leigh W. Hart's **Heal, Grow, & Thrive** book series offers accessible, research-backed guidance on personal development and emotional healing. Titles like **Reparenting Your Wounded Inner Child** and **CBT Inner Child Workbook** provide step-by-step approaches to addressing childhood trauma and building emotional resilience.

While **The Ultimate Shadow Work Journal & Workbook** serves as a powerful tool for deep self-exploration, guiding readers through transformative inner work to uncover hidden emotions and patterns.

"With each book, I release my work into the world, infused with positive energy, hoping it reaches those who need it most. The transformative potential of books to inspire change is what drives me to pour my heart into every word I write." ~Leigh W. Hart

Amazon.com/Author/LeighWHart

My Gift to You!

Customized Worksheets:

Elevate your journey with a **customized collection** of **110+ journal pages and interactive worksheets** that have been designed to complement the steps, journal prompts, and exercises discussed in this book perfectly.

Bonus #1

BENEFITS:

- Print multiple copies of repeatable exercises.
- Create a private journal with the book's 150+ prompts.
- Increase your commitment to the exercises.
- Counselors, therapists, and coaches can share printed copies with clients.

Go to:

SelfLove.LeighWHart.com

to receive your BONUS printable support materials.

My Gift to You!

Mastering the Art of Time Management Workbook:

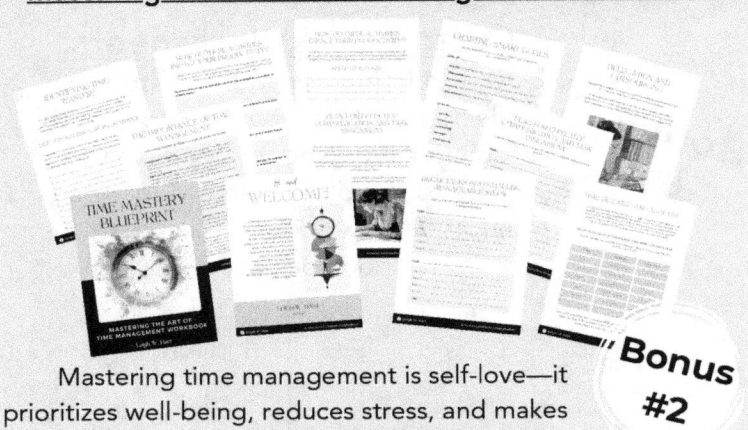

Mastering time management is self-love—it prioritizes well-being, reduces stress, and makes room for rest, growth, and fulfilling activities.

Bonus #2

The Wheel of Life Workbook:

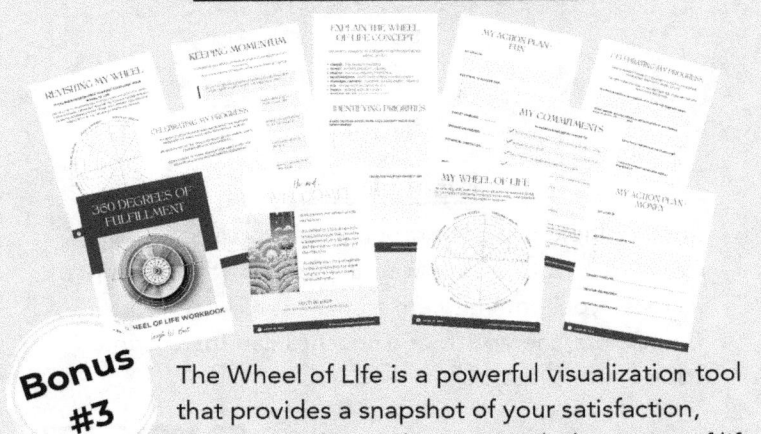

Bonus #3

The Wheel of LIfe is a powerful visualization tool that provides a snapshot of your satisfaction, balance, and growth across eight key areas of life.

Go to:
SelfLove.LeighWHart.com
to receive your BONUS printable support materials.

REFERENCES

Ackerman, C. (2019, July 10). *23 amazing health benefits of mindfulness for body and brain.* PositivePsychology.com. https://positivepsychology.com/benefits-of-mindfulness/

Ancverina, A. (2024, September). *Common misconceptions about art therapy: A therapist's perspective on working with children and young adults.* TRC | London | Edinburgh | Riyadh. https://trcgroup.org.uk/common-misconceptions-about-art-therapy-a-therapists-perspective-on-working-with-children-and-young-adults

Angelou, M. (n.d.). Maya Angelou quote. Goodreads. https://www.goodreads.com/quotes/512-there-is-no-greater-agony-than-bearing-an-untold-story

Black, D., & Slavich, G. (2016). Mindfulness meditation and the immune system: a systematic review of randomized controlled trials. *Annals of the New York Academy of Sciences, 1373*(1), 13–24. https://doi.org/10.1111/nyas.12998

Bjarnadottir, A. (2023, January 4). *Mindful eating 101 — A beginner's guide.* Healthline; Healthline Media. https://www.healthline.com/nutrition/mindful-eating-guide

Bobby, J. (2022, August 15). *Mental health benefits of coloring.* Mayo Clinic Health System. https://www.mayoclinichealthsystem.org/hometown-health/speaking-of-health/coloring-is-good-for-your-health

Bowden, T. (2024, May 24). Brushing away stress: 21 art therapy activities for self-expression and healing. *RMCAD.* https://www.rmcad.edu/blog/brushing-away-stress-21-art-therapy-activities-for-self-expression-and-healing/

Campbell, E. (2018, February 13). *How photography can help cultivate mindfulness and gratitude.* Greater Good. https://greatergood.berkeley.edu/article/item/how_photography_can_help_cultivate_mindfulness_and_gratitude

Casabianca, S. (2024, November 22). *15 cognitive distortions to blame for your negative thinking.* Psych Central. https://psychcentral.com/lib/cognitive-distortions-negative-thinking

Celestine, N. (2020, August 15). *What is mindful breathing? Exercises, scripts and videos.* PositivePsychology. https://positivepsychology.com/mindful-breathing/

Charlie Health Editorial Team. (2023, April 11). *FAST: A DBT skill for maintaining your self-respect.* Charlie Health. https://www.charliehealth.com/post/fast-a-dbt-skill

Chapman, G. (2024). *Gary Chapman* quote. Goodreads. https://www.goodreads. com/quotes/328589-love-is-a-choice-you-make-everyday

Cherry, K. (2023, November 9). *How art therapy is used to help people heal.* Verywell Mind. https://www.verywellmind.com/what-is-art-therapy-2795755

Cirino, E. (2024, June 6). *10 Tips to Help You Stop Ruminating.* Healthline. https:// www.healthline.com/health/how-to-stop-ruminating

Clarke, J. (2024, December 4). *How narrative therapy works.* Verywell Mind. https:// www.verywellmind.com/narrative-therapy-4172956

Color psychology: The psychological effects of colors. (n.d.). *Art Therapy.* http:// www.arttherapyblog.com/online/color-psychology-psychologica-effects-of-colors/

Craig, D. (2024, April 9). *The stories we tell ourselves: Unlocking your inner narrative.* Linkedin.com. https://www.linkedin.com/pulse/stories-we-tell-ourselves-unlocking-your-inner-narrative-craig-8wvzc

Cronkleton, E. (2024, May 17). *10 breathing techniques.* Healthline. https://www. healthline.com/health/breathing-exercise

Cuncic, A. (2024, June 13). *What Is Radical Acceptance?* Verywell Mind. https://www. verywellmind.com/what-is-radical-acceptance-5120614

DBT : TIPP - skills, worksheets, videos, & activities. (2024, February 11). DBT. https:// dialecticalbehaviortherapy.com/distress-tolerance/tipp/

Distract with wise mind ACCEPTS. (2024). Dbtselfhelp.com. https://dbtselfhelp.com/ distract-with-wise-mind-accepts/

Felman, A. (2023, October 27). *Stress: Why does it happen and how can we manage it?* Www.medicalnewstoday.com. https://www.medicalnewstoday.com/articles/ 145855#types

Find your inner safe space . (2019, January 24). Self-Love Rainbow. https://www.self loverainbow.com/find-your-inner-safe-space/

Godreau, J. (2024, June 12). *9 amazing therapeutic benefits of art for anxiety management.* Mindful Health Solutions. https://mindfulhealthsolutions.com/9-amaz ing-therapeutic-benefits-of-art-for-anxiety-management/

Goyal, M., Singh, S., Sibinga, E. M. S., Gould, N. F., Rowland-Seymour, A., Sharma, R., Berger, Z., Sleicher, D., Maron, D. D., Shihab, H. M., Ranasinghe, P. D., Linn, S., Saha, S., Bass, E. B., & Haythornthwaite, J. A. (2014). Meditation programs for psychological stress and well-being. *JAMA Internal Medicine, 174*(3), 357. https:// doi.org/10.1001/jamainternmed.2013.13018

Gupta, S. (2024, April 29). *Feeling anxious? Try the 5-4-3-2-1 grounding technique.* Verywell Mind. https://www.verywellmind.com/5-4-3-2-1-grounding-tech nique-8639390

Hematian, F., & Moraveji, M. (2023). The effectiveness of mindfulness based stress reduction training on increasing of emotional intelligence, job satisfaction and mental health of a petroleum employees. *Journal of Adolescent and Youth Psychological Studies (JAYPS)*, 4(9), 142–154. https://doi.org/10.61838/kman. jayps.4.9.16

Hemrajani, K. (n.d.). *What is normal stress and bad stress?* Common Care. https://www.commoncarecentral.com/mental-health-a-to-z/whats-normal-stress-and-bad-stress

Hesse, H. (n.d.). *Hermann Hesse quote.* Goodreads. https://www.goodreads.com/quotes/7540208-within-you-there-is-a-stillness-and-a-sanctuary-to

Hibbert, C. (2014, January 8). *Discovering self-worth: Why is it so hard to love ourselves?* Dr.ChristinaHibbert. https://www.drchristinahibbert.com/discovering-self-worth-why-is-it-so-hard-to-love-ourselves/

Hillesum, E. (n.d.). *Etty Hillesum quote.* Goodreads. https://www.goodreads.com/quotes/578519-sometimes-the-most-important-thing-in-a-whole-day-is

Hofmann, S. G., Sawyer, A. T., Witt, A. A., & Oh, D. (2010). The effect of mindfulness-based therapy on anxiety and depression: A meta-analytic review. *Journal of Consulting and Clinical Psychology*, 78(2), 169–183. https://doi.org/10.1037/a0018555

Holland, K. (2023, March 16). *Amygdala hijack: When emotion takes over.* Healthline; Healthline Media. https://www.healthline.com/health/stress/amygdala-hijack

How to love yourself: Self love for beginners. (2022, September 6). Sage & Bloom. https://sageandbloom.co/how-to-love-yourself-self-love-for-beginners/

Hutchinson, T. (n.d.). *Why are personal boundaries important?* Tracy Hutchinson, PhD | Fort Myers Therapy. https://www.drtracyhutchinson.com/what-are-personal-boundaries-and-why-are-they-important/

Jaime. (2023, July 11). Creating your perfect meditation space. *Balanceapp.com.* https://balanceapp.com/blog/crafting-your-ideal-meditation-space

Kabat-Zinn, J. (n.d.). *Mindfulness body scan by Jon Kabat-Zinn.* Mindfulness Training. https://mbsrtraining.com/mindfulness-body-scan-by-jon-kabat-zinn/

Kabat-Zinn, J. (2018, November 8). *This loving-kindness meditation is a radical act of love.* Mindful. https://www.mindful.org/this-loving-kindness-meditation-is-a-radical-act-of-love/

Katielips. (2022, July 21). *The four pillars of self-love.* Thrive Global. https://community.thriveglobal.com/the-four-pillars-of-self-love/

Kriakous, S. A., Elliott, K. A., Lamers, C., & Owen, R. (2020). The effectiveness of mindfulness-based stress reduction on the psychological functioning of healthcare professionals: A systematic review. *Mindfulness*, 12(1), 1–28. https://doi.org/10.1007/s12671-020-01500-9

Kuyken, W. (2024, December 11). Coming home to your body. *Psychology Today.* https://www.psychologytoday.com/ca/blog/mindfulness/202412/coming-home-to-your-body

Lewis, C. S. (n.d.). *C. S. Lewis quote*. Goodreads. https://www.goodreads.com/quotes/10348517-you-can-t-go-back-and-change-the-beginning-but-you

Linehan, M. (2015). *DBT® skills training manual*. Psycnet.apa.org. https://psycnet.apa.org/record/2015-05780-000

Linehan, M. (2024). *Emotional regulation skills*. Dialectical Behavior Therapy (DBT) Tools. https://dbt.tools/emotional_regulation/index.php

Ma, X., Yue, Z.-Q., Gong, Z.-Q., Zhang, H., Duan, N.-Y., Shi, Y.-T., Wei, G.-X., & Li, Y.-F. (2017). The effect of diaphragmatic breathing on attention, negative affect and stress in healthy adults. *Frontiers in Psychology, 8*(874), 1–12. https://doi.org/10.3389/fpsyg.2017.00874

Marie, S. (2022, October 27). *9 tips for respecting other people's boundaries*. Psych Central. https://psychcentral.com/relationships/how-to-respect-other-peoples-boundaries

Mayer, B. A. (2022, February 14). *Could mindfulness-based stress reduction help you find calm?* Healthline. https://www.healthline.com/health/mindfulness-based-stress-reduction

Merton, T. (n.d.). *Thomas Merton quote*. Goodreads. https://www.goodreads.com/quotes/7942175-art-enables-us-to-find-ourselves-and-lose-ourselves-at

Mind-Body connection: The role of meditation and mindfulness. (2023, July 12). Life Coach Certification Online. https://lifecoachtraining.co/mind-body-connection-the-role-of-meditation-and-mindfulness/

Mindful Staff. (2020, July 8). *What is mindfulness?* Mindful. https://www.mindful.org/what-is-mindfulness/

Mohsin, M. (2024, October 8). *The cognitive and emotional benefits of writing: How journaling and creative writing improve mental health, especially in managing anxiety and depression*. Medium. https://minahil14.medium.com/the-cognitive-and-emotional-benefits-of-writing-how-journaling-and-creative-writing-improve-mental-9414f1529388

Murakami, H. (n.d.). *Haruki Murakami quote*. Goodreads. https://www.goodreads.com/quotes/613585-pain-is-inevitable-suffering-is-optional-say-you-re-running-and

Picasso, P. (n.d.). *Pablo Picasso quote*. Goodreads. https://www.goodreads.com/quotes/4673-art-washes-away-from-the-soul-the-dust-of-everyday

Rainey, J. (2024, July 19). *The connection between art and mental health*. Jennarainey.com. https://jennarainey.com/connection-between-art-and-mental-health/

Relationship effectiveness: GIVE . (n.d.). DBT Self Help. https://dbtselfhelp.com/relationship-effectiveness-give/

Rosenzweig, S., Greeson, J. M., Reibel, D. K., Green, J. S., Jasser, S. A., & Beasley, D. (2010). Mindfulness-based stress reduction for chronic pain conditions:

Variation in treatment outcomes and role of home meditation practice. *Journal of Psychosomatic Research, 68*(1), 29–36. https://doi.org/10.1016/j.jpsychores.2009.03.010

Roy Chowdhury, M. (2019, October 22). *15 music therapy activities and tools.* PositivePsychology.com. https://positivepsychology.com/music-therapy-activities-tools/

Rumi J. (n.d.). Jalal ad-Din Muhammad ar-Rumi Quote. Goodreads. https://www.goodreads.com/quotes/9726-your-task-is-not-to-seek-for-love-but-merely

Runion, L. (2023, August 1). *Examples of negative self-talk that are keeping you stuck (and how to stop).* Loren Runion. https://lorenrunion.com/examples-of-negative-self-talk/

Schimelpfening, N. (2023, November 2). *Dialectical behavior therapy (DBT): Definition, techniques, and benefits.* Verywell Mind. https://www.verywellmind.com/dialectical-behavior-therapy-1067402

Scott, E. (2024, February 12). *What is body scan meditation?* Verywell Mind. https://www.verywellmind.com/body-scan-meditation-why-and-how-3144782

Serina. (2023, May 18). *How to use color to convey emotion in art.* Https://Www.doodlersanonymous.com/. https://www.doodlersanonymous.com/how-to-use-color-to-convey-emotion-in-art/

Shamsi, H. (2020, October 23). Keep calm and doodle on: The cognitive and mental health benefits of doodling. *Blog.well-Nest.ca.* https://blog.well-nest.ca/2020/10/22/cognitive-and-mental-health-benefits-of-doodling/

Stewart, A. (2023, March 30). *13 habits of self-love every woman should adopt.* Healthline. https://www.healthline.com/health/13-self-love-habits-every-woman-needs-to-have

Stress. (2022, January 25). Www.healthdirect.gov.au. https://www.healthdirect.gov.au/stress#symptoms

Sutton, J. (2020, July 15). *What is mindful walking meditation and how can it impact your life?* PositivePsychology.com. https://positivepsychology.com/mindful-walking/

Sutton, J. (2024, July 12). *Urge surfing: How riding the wave breaks bad habits.* PositivePsychology.com. https://positivepsychology.com/urge-surfing/

Tiwari, D. (2023, November 6). *3 types of stress: Causes, effects, & how to cope.* Choosing Therapy. https://www.choosingtherapy.com/types-of-stress/

Visvanathan, P. (2024). 5 Minutes of Mindful Stretching. In *Insighttimer.com.* https://insighttimer.com/visvanathan/guided-meditations/5-minutes-of-mindful-stretching

Ware, K. (2019, March 6). *3 ways to train your mindfulness muscle.* Kristy Ware. https://kristyware.com/3-ways-to-train-your-mindfulness-muscle/

Weathering the storm through distress tolerance training. (2024, May 10). Houston DBT Center. https://houstondbtcenter.com/distress-tolerance-training/

Yoga, D. (2018, January 24). *Guided object meditation: Mindfulness into no mind.* Doron Yoga - Doron Yoga Academy. https://doronyoga.com/guided-object-meditation-mindfulness-into-no-mind/

Zen proverb quote. (n.d.). Goodreads. https://www.goodreads.com/author/quotes/6880875.Zen_Proverb

Image References

Images on the following pages were created with the assistance of Midjourney: 16, 23, 49, 55, 116, 143, 154, 190, 212, 219

Lightning Source LLC
Chambersburg PA
CBHW061735120626
46550CB00005B/1801